Viola

Herb of the Year™ 2022

International Herb Association

Compiled and edited by Kathleen Connole

IHA HERB OF THE YEAR™

Each year the International Herb Association chooses an **Herb of the Year**™ to highlight. The Horticultural Committee evaluates possible choices based on their being outstanding in at least two of the three major categories: culinary, medicinal, and ornamental. Herbal organizations around the world work together with us to educate the public throughout the year.

Herb of the Year™ books are published annually by the

International Herb Association
P.O. Box 5667 Jacksonville, Florida 32247-5667
www.iherb.org

This book is intended as an informational guide. The remedies, approaches, and techniques described herein are meant to supplement, and not to be a substitute for professional medical care or treatment; please consult your health care provider.

The International Herb Association is a professional trade organization providing education, service, and development for members engaged in all aspects of the herbal industry.

ISBN: 978-0-578-36029-4

*Uniting Herb Professionals for Growth
Through Promotion and Education*

The International Herb Association has some of the most dedicated volunteers who keep the organization afloat, giving their time and talents to ensure that IHA continues to share herbal knowledge and connect those in the profession of herbs. We are deeply indebted to the IHA Board of Directors, the IHA Foundation members, and our webmaster. Thanks for all that you do and for caring enough to move us forward!

Acknowledgments

It has been my good fortune to happen to become editor of the Herb of the Year™ book when the chosen herb is *Viola*, such a cheerful group of flowers that seem to be loved by all.

I would like to thank all the contributors who responded so enthusiastically with a wonderful variety of topics.

Thanks to **Susan Belsinger** for continuing **Art Tucker's** tradition of covering botany and cultural information, by including the article on *Viola* that they wrote together. More helpful tips on growing violets and pansies from seed are provided by **Theresa Mieseler, Tina Marie Wilcox,** and **Deb Jolly. Deb Jolly** also introduces us to a very unusual member of the *Viola* genus. **Karen O'Brien** covers *Viola* species native to North America and their traditional medicinal uses. An interesting and fun article on violets and children by **Susan Betz** and **Chuck Voigt's** sweet *Viola* memories complete the section on Knowing and Growing.

Violets in the Kitchen contains a wide variety of recipes using violets. Thanks to **Susan Belsinger, Pat Crocker, Karen England, Donna Frawley, Cooper T. Murray,** and **Phyllis Williams** for so many delicious ways to enjoy violets, showing us that they are pleasing to our eyes as well as our taste buds.

Violets have been a favorite subject in Art, Literature, and Poetry and **Gert Coleman, Pat Crocker,** and **Skye Suter** have given us some wonderful examples to enjoy.

The medicinal uses of violets are covered extensively by **Daniel Gagnon,** and **Dorene Petersen** with **Glen Nagel; Carol Little** shares her knowledge of violets as medicine as well. There are lovely recipes for ways to use violets for health and beauty by **Janice Cox, Marge Powell,** and **Jane Stevens. Gail Wood Miller** beautifully explains her perspective on the healing properties of violets.

Thanks to **Susan Belsinger** for her *Viola* haikus, little gems scattered throughout the book. **Jane Stevens'** poem closes *Viola Herb of the Year™ 2022* and leaves us smiling.

The gloriously colorful photographs of all kinds and colors of *Viola* have been provided by **Susan Belsinger, Heather Cohen, Gert Coleman, Deb Jolly**, and **Pat Kenny**. Delicious photographs that accompany recipes were provided by **Susan Belsinger, Karen England, Donna Frawley, Cooper T. Murray, Jane Stevens**, and **Phyllis Williams**. Photos to accompany how-to articles were provided by **Deb Jolly, Janice Cox, Marge Powell**, and **Tina Marie Wilcox**.

Great admiration goes to our very creative illustrators, **Deborah Hall, Pat Kenny, Alicia Mann, Skye Suter**, and **Gail Wood Miller**.

Words cannot express adequately the gratitude for the help that was given by **Susan Belsinger** and **Gert Coleman** as second readers and editorial advisors with infinite patience.

Many thanks to the incredibly talented **Heather Cohen**, who takes all the pieces and puts them together into something that is so much more than the sum of its parts, an amazing feat!

I would like thank the IHA Foundation and Board for all that they do to support and promote this very worthwhile organization. I greatly appreciate the Board's encouragement and confidence in my abilities.

Finally, I would like to thank my family members who have cheered me on in this new endeavor; especially husband **Jeffrey** for being my support system and helping in so many little ways to make life easier.

~Kathleen Connole, Editor

Viola

Herb of the Year™

2022

Pat Kenny

Table of Contents

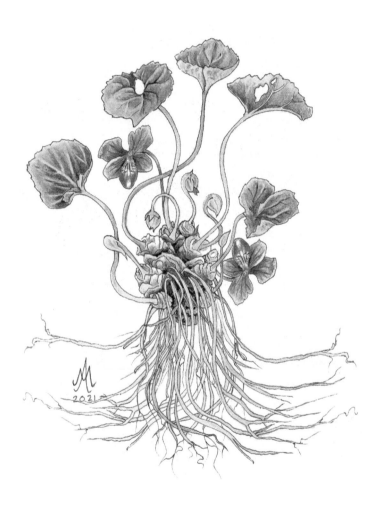

Alicia Mann

Knowing & Growing Viola

Dew-kissed violets: common blue violet, Confederate violet and 'Freckles'.
Susan Belsinger

Viola species from *The Culinary Herbal*

Susan Belsinger & Arthur O. Tucker

Happy little faces of viola blossoms are harbingers of spring. These common European wildflowers are traditionally used to garnish the May wine punch bowl and other beverages, desserts, tea sandwiches, and salads. They are used in making jellies, butters, and fancy desserts. The wild violets are separated in this discussion from the Johnny-jump-ups (*Viola tricolor*) and pansies, since they are generally found naturalized in the wild, in contrast to cultivated perennials. While all the colorful little blooms in this genus are safe to eat, the foliage of wild violets is edible whereas the leaves of "johnnies" and pansies are not eaten.

Wild violets

Violets or *Viola* species most often refer to the wild purple-blue violets, *Viola sororia* (sometimes called *V. papilionacea* in the older literature), or the white-flowering wood or Confederate violets, *V. sororia forma priceana*. Other common wild species are the birdfoot violet, *V. pedata* (also called bird-foot, birdsfoot, or bird's foot) and sweet violets, *V. odorata*. Wild violet leaves are usually heart-shaped, except for the birdfoot, whose leaves look like what its name suggests. Violet blooms have five petals, which are held up on long, thin stems above the foliage. The first two violets have a mild scent, slightly sweet, and the taste is also very mild, sometimes a touch acidic. Sweet violet (*V. odorata*), however, is very fragrant with a strong, sweet perfume and tastes much more flowery. Generally, flowers with the stronger fragrance have more flavor, so they are used in beverages, syrups, cordials, pastilles, ice creams, and confections. They are also often candied and used to garnish fancy desserts.

Violet flowers and young leaves are eaten raw in salads; they contain a good amount of vitamins A and C. Leaves are cooked with other spring greens or added to stews as a thickening agent, since they have a slight mucilaginous quality. If eaten in large amounts, because of the saponin content, viola may cause nausea and a tonic cleansing effect.

Johnny-jump-up or heartsease (*V. tricolor*); pansy (*V. ×wittrockiana*)

Generally, all of the Johnny-jump-ups blooms taste like a mild salad green, some with a hint of perfume. Both Johnny-jump-ups and pansies (*V. ×wittrockiana*) have a pleasing mild, sweet taste like baby lettuce. Some of them have a slight, mild hint of wintergreen, and a few bring bubblegum to mind. Smell and taste the blooms before using. We love the faces of these flowers and the huge variety of color combinations. Use them on salads: the whole bloom of Johnny-jump-ups and pansies can be used or pull the petals from the calyx and sprinkle them on salads or canapés. The colored petals are lovely in herb butter, floating on a beverage, or scattered on frosted cakes or cupcakes. The flowers can be candied and used as a fancy edible garnish on desserts or as a confection. They are also quite lovely adorning May wine or embedded in an ice ring.

Growing Basics

biennials to perennials, 4 to 12 inches tall
violets hardy to zone 5; pansies and heartsease hardy to zone 8
sun, part shade;
pansies and heartsease need part shade in hot climates
keep moist but not wet
fertile, well-drained soil, pH 6.5 to 7.0

Cultivation and propagation

Viola species grow best in a woodland environment. They favor shade to partial shade, though they will perform well in a sunny, herbaceous border with proper moisture and organic matter. Plants do not get much larger than 6 to 12 inches tall. The violet is a hardy perennial with large heart-shaped leaves and blooms in various shades of purple and white with purple veins. They are naturalized in lawns, fields, and woodland edges and will spread if allowed to do so.

Pansies and "johnnies" can be started from seed, and plants are widely available at garden centers and nurseries. Pansies are biennials to short-lived perennials but are most often treated as an annual. Their blooms come in many colors, from white, yellow, orange, pink, lavender, and purple, to bi- and tri-colored. The short-lived perennial Johnny-jump-up, also known as heartsease, is usually lavender, purple, white, or yellow, or a combination thereof; their flowers are about the size of violets. They often self-sow and will reappear in your garden every spring.

Harvesting and preserving

Leaves of violets (not "johnnies" or pansies) can be harvested, washed and spun dry, and used like a salad green or cooked. They can also be dried for use in tea or soups. Pick viola flowers and put their stems in water until ready to use. Pinch the flowers from the stems and use small flowers whole. Use pansies whole as a garnish or separate the petals to scatter them. Violets and Johnny-jump-ups are ideal for candying—which is the best way to preserve the bloom for eating—although they do press well in a flower press for crafting. Store candied blooms in a tightly closed container between layers of wax paper or parchment paper up to about six months.

Making violet tincture. *Susan Belsinger*

Susan Belsinger teaches, lectures, and writes about gardening and cooking, and is a food writer, editor and photographer who has authored and edited over 25 books and hundreds of articles. Recently referred to as a "flavor artist", Susan delights in kitchen alchemy—the blending of harmonious foods, herbs, and spices—to create real, delicious food, as well as libations, that nourish our bodies and spirits and titillate our senses.

She was the editor for the International Herb Association's Herb of the Year books from 2007 to 2012. Susan was the Otto Richter Award recipient in 2009 and received the IHA award for Outstanding Contributions to the Herb Industry in 2004. She was Honorary President of the Herb Society of America for the 2018 to 2020 term. Her latest publication is *Grow Your Own Herbs*, co-authored with Arthur O. Tucker, Timber Press, 2019. Susan delights in each new herb of the year: doing research, growing the specimens, taking photos, creating recipes, sharing her findings and celebrating the plants. www.susanbelsinger.com

Susan Belsinger speaks of Art Tucker:
Ever since I began working on contributing to and editing the IHA's Herb of the Year books with the first one being <u>Oregano, Herb of the Year, 2005</u>, *I requested that Art Tucker contribute information on growing from* <u>The Big Book of Herbs</u>, *co-authored with Thomas DeBaggio, Interweave Press, 2000. Art always willingly contributed to each Herb of the Year book and in 2009 the Tucker & DeBaggio book was revised and reprinted by Timber Press as* <u>The Encyclopedia of Herbs</u> *and the annual contribution came from the newer version thereafter.* <u>Hops, Herb of the Year 2018</u> *was the last year that our dear Art contributed from that encyclopedic source.*

With Art's passing and Covid, I fumbled through the thicket (no Rubus entry in <u>The Encyclopedia of Herbs</u>) *and did an article for* <u>Rubus, Herb of the Year 2020</u> *on the brambles. I decided to carry on the Tucker tradition of contributing to HOY (I know he would approve) and so for* <u>Parsley, Herb of the Year 2021</u> *and now* <u>Viola, Herb of the Year 2022</u>, *I have contributed growing information from our book,* <u>The Culinary Herbal</u>, *which we co-authored together, Timber Press, 2016. I will continue to carry on the tradition as long as there is an Herb of the Year and I have information on the subject at hand.* ~S.B.

African Violets Are Not Violas

Susan Belsinger

When I typed in "violets" to do a search, more hits for African violets came up before any other violets (*Viola* spp.) appeared.

So, I figured that it was best to let the general public know that African violets are in no way related to the genus *Viola*! They were so called because the bloom is somewhat similar in appearance (well perhaps at first glance for the untrained eye), they both have five petals, and they do both have heart-shaped leaves. Otherwise, as you will read below, there are no other similarities.

The genus name of African violets is *Saintpaulia* and there are six species of these flowering plants in the Gesneriaceae family. The genus name comes from the German official, Baron Walter von Saint Paul-Illaire, who is said to have collected the first of these plants in 1892, in German East Africa which is now Tanzania. African violets (*S. ionantha*) are tropical plants, found growing in Eastern Africa, especially Tanzania and Kenya, in the higher altitudes.

These small, herbaceous perennials have thick, dark green leaves which are quite hirsute (very hairy). The somewhat ovate leaves come from the base of the plant in a basal cluster, borne on long petioles (stems of the leaves). The blooms, which are like a viola bloom with five petals, are bilaterally symmetrical, whereas a viola does not have petals all the same size. And the blooms are borne on small panicles above the leaves, while common violets have no leaves on their flower stem. Just like the *Viola* (Violaceae family) that they are named for, they can be violet, purple, pale blue, white or pink in color; otherwise, there is no relationship to *Viola* species.

African violets have long been a popular houseplant and there are now hundreds of varieties developed for their shapes and colors—some are trailing—and there is a whole slew of miniatures (which are quite darling). They are long-lived with a lifespan of up to 50 years, easy to grow; they bloom throughout the year, and it is easy to propagate them from leaf cuttings.

African violet flowers are very different from violas—their blooms are bilaterally symmetrical while violas do not have petals that are the same size—leaves grow from a basal cluster, are very hirsute and ovate.
Susan Belsinger

A well-drained growing medium is of utmost importance—a common soilless mix is 3 parts sphagnum peat moss, 2 parts vermiculite and 1 part perlite—this is sold in garden nurseries as African violet mix. The crown must be set above the surface of the growing medium, and plants are watered from the bottom, so they need saucers, or there are special African violet containers that are like a shallow pot within a pot (not deep). Plants will perish if overwatered, though they do not like to be dried out; there is a balance that you will figure out if cultivating *Saintpaulia ionantha.*

They do require good light, though it can indirect or artificial—I've seen them thrive in office situations with no natural light. My grandmother grew a whole bay window full of African violets in her dining room. which received midday sun. They flourished under her care and she always had little glass custard cups with foil across the top; she poked a hole in the foil and stuck a leaf stem in the water to propagate them. My mother continues the tradition and even has one of Mema's violets still going. She grows large specimens on her kitchen counter, where they get indirect sunlight from the window over the sink; however, they need to be turned in natural light situations or they will rapidly become asymmetrical in shape. I have never seen Mom's violets without blooms; in the right conditions they will bloom continually (she does give them African violet plant food and cleans their leaves regularly). They like to be warm like in Mom's kitchen—humidity is fine—however no cold drafts or they will perish!

I have two African violets—one is from a piece of my grandmother's violet and the other I inherited from my mother-in-law. They are many years old and rather neglected, located on a shelf in indirect light, so I have to turn them, or they get lopsided. My house is heated by a woodstove, so they get covered with soot and dust; I rinse them off occasionally even though they don't like to get their leaves wet. I usually water them from the top (considered a no-no) and although they need repotting badly, they keep blooming their little hearts out.

Now that you understand some of the characteristics of the African violet, you know that they are nowhere near related to the *Viola* which grows wild in our gardens and lawns. While we can eat both the leaves and flowers of the common violets, *African violets are not edible.* The latest news is, after recent genetic studies, taxonomists have decided that *Saintpaulia* belongs to the genus *Streptocarpus.* So, the new and correct botanical name for African violets is *Streptocarpus ionanthus.*

In the herbal blog https://laidbackgardener.blog/2018/01/29/the-african-violet-changes-its-name/, author Larry Hodgson states: "Theoretically, you should therefore call your African violet *Streptocarpus* subgenus *Streptocarpella* sect. *Saintpaulia*… That means the species from which most African violet cultivars are derived, *Saintpaulia ionantha*, officially becomes *Streptocarpus* sect. *Saintpaulia ionanthus* (note that *ionantha* becomes *ionanthus* to match the gender of *Streptocarpus*), or much more simply, just *Streptocarpus ionanthus*."

Both the Gesneriad Society and the African Violet Society of America (international registration authority for *Saintpaulia*) have accepted this name change and will be transitioning to the use of *Streptocarpus* as the genus name for what has been *Saintpaulia*. According to The Gesneriad Reference Web: "It's important to recognize that *Saintpaulia* remains a legitimate botanical name, as a Section within *Streptocarpus* subgenus *Streptocarpella* and references to *Saintpaulia* remain valid as long as this is understood."

References

https://www.gesneriads.info/articles/saintpaulia/saintpaulia/taxonomy/species-names-use/. Accessed June 11.

Hodgson, Larry. "The African Violet Changes Its Name." *Laidback Gardener*. https://www.laidbackgardener.blog/2018/01/29/the-african-violet-changes-its-name/. Accessed 6/11/21.

https://www.britannica.com/plant/African-violet. Accessed June 11, 2021

HTTPS://WWW.GOOGLE.COM/SEARCH?CLIENT=FIREFOX-B-1-D&Q=BOTANICAL+NAME+FOR+AFRICAN+VIOLETS#KPFB-STAGE=1&KPFB-TATTR=&KPFB-FTYPE=1. Accessed June 11, 2021.

https://www.missouribotanicalgarden.org/PlantFinder/PlantFinderDetails.aspx?kempercode=b567. Accessed June 11, 2021.

https://www.serenataflowers.com/pollennation/flower-history-origin/. Accessed June 11, 2021.

Susan Belsinger Bio on page 6

Pansies, Violas & Violets:
A Child's Perspective

Susan Betz

The plants closest to you are those from your childhood;
those are the ones you truly love.
V.S. Naipul

Violets, pansies, and Johnny-jump-ups are among the most treasured of all our wild and garden flowers, charming children and grown-ups alike for centuries in a shared delight. Botanically speaking, violets, pansies, and Johnny-jump-ups belong to the Violaceae family and genus *Viola*. There are 500 to 600 *Viola* species worldwide, and of those, 127 species are native to the United States. Pansies are descendants of the small Johnny-jump-up, affectionately called heartsease, introduced into America from Europe. In the 1830s, breeders started crossing Johnny-jump-ups, *V. tricolor,* with the related plant *Viola lutea* and came up with the pansy, nicknamed "the stepmother" and botanically named *Viola* x*wittrockiana.* The x means they originated as hybrids.

If a flower is passed along to us with many common names, it's a sure sign children have loved it. Common blue violets are known by numerous nicknames and Johnny-jump-ups have close to one hundred. If you look at a list of flowers recommended for children's gardens, you will always find members of *Viola* included on the list. Pansies and wild violets are favorites. They are all easy to grow from seed or starts and thrive in wildflower gardens or cultivated settings. They are tolerant of youthful curiosity, a bit of horticultural negligence, and are useful for many fun activities in and out of the garden.

Violets are low-growing herbaceous perennials with attractive heart-shaped leaves and dark purple or white flowers with purple variegations. The flowers and leaves grow directly from underground rhizomes, which form small colonies. The purple violet, *V. sororia,* is the most common, but you can also

Fritillaries Eat Violets

1. GREAT SPANGLED FRITILLARY 2. G.S. FRITILLARY PUPA
3. EASTERN MEADOW FRITILLARY 4. E.M. FRITILLARY LARVA
5. E.M. FRITILLARY PUPA 6. G.S. FRITILLARY LARVA

Fritallaries and violets. *Deborah Hall*

find white and pink varieties growing wild. The violet produces two sorts of flowers. Everyone knows the bright colored flowers, but later in the season, these are followed by others that seem like seedpods or buds that never open. Many gardeners consider the common blue violet's vigorous growing habit too aggressive, while others value this characteristic and utilize it to solve tough landscape situations.

Violets grow best in sunny or lightly shaded locations with moist to average soils. The common blue violet returns each spring about the same time as the redbud tree begins to bloom, and they are frequently found growing in the same vicinity. Another similarity shared by the redbud trees and violets is their heart-shaped leaves and edible flowers.

Johnny-jump-ups, or heartsease, are carefree biennial plants with erect stems covered with cheerful small flowers of blue, yellow, and white. They freely self-seed.

Pansies are annuals with large flowers up to 3 inches across with blotchy markings and one, two, or three colors. Children naturally love pansies because their flowers resemble human faces—some seem to smile, another might have a sad face or plucky expression and others are plain, honest, or happy. The similarity to a face is not as apparent to a grown-up, because they are not low enough to look a pansy straight in the eye.

Children grasp a large body of valuable knowledge about plants by playing and experimenting with their leaves, roots, flowers, and stems. What's more, they become more observant of the life cycles of local plants, insects and their responses to seasonal change, weather, and climate. Our sense of place is established not only by the "place", but our relationship to it, and is dependent on our firsthand knowledge of and experience with that place. An old plant proverb states "he who bends a knee where violets grow, a hundred secret things shall know."

According to data taken in 1890, 1937, and 1959, children were asked to rate their favorite games and pastimes. Play with plants topped the list in 1890 but sadly disappeared by 1959.

These are some intriguing adaptations and interactions violas have with their wildlife friends that children can readily observe. When cold temperatures or unpredictable weather prevent insects from pollinating the violets' pretty blue flowers in spring, the plant produces tiny inconspicuous self-pollinating flowers hidden beneath leaves close to the ground to ensure seed production for the next year. This type of flower gets its name, *cleistogamous*, from two Greek words meaning "closed marriage," and these flowers are found in almost all violet species.

Violets have multiple methods of reproducing, including vegetatively by underground stems or rhizomes, self-seeding, and mutualism! Here is how that works: ants prize the sweet outer shell of the seeds as treats. They carry them back to their nests, eat the coverings, and help plant the seeds when they discard the seeds in the soil beneath the ground. Both the plant and the ants benefit from this relationship. Curiously, farmer ants help disperse more than thirty percent of spring-flowering herbaceous plants growing in eastern North America.

Violets are the caterpillar host plant for the Great Spangled and Lesser Fritillary butterflies. The *Viola* genus supports twenty-nine butterfly and moth species. Violets are not a highly favored nectar and pollen source for many insects, like some of our other spring wildflowers, but they do attract native bees and syrphid flies.

Humans are not the only ones who crave fresh green spring vegetation. Cutworms, the larva of noctuid moths, cut the violet leaves off and eat them; slugs chew irregular shaped holes in the leaves at night and hide beneath the leaves during the day.

The flowers and leaves of violets have been used for food, medicine, and play since ancient times. Wild plant foragers value violets as a healthy spring green in salads and tonics because of their high levels of vitamin C. In addition, violet flowers are used to make candy, jam, and herbal syrups. During medieval times syrup made from violet flowers was commonly used as a laxative for infants and children. Native Americans used violet rhizomes to make an insect-repelling infusion for soaking seed corn before planting.

Viola flowers have a wealth of lovely poems, legends, and plant lore associated with their origins. The violet symbolizes constancy and modesty, and its history dates to ancient Greece and Rome. The name *pansy* is a corruption of the French word *pensée,* meaning thoughts, and pansies have long been associated with thoughts of love.

Every plant has a story to tell and the more common the plant is, the more stories, myths, and legends it seems to have, and the violet is no exception. Sharing a plant's folklore and natural history is a fun way to introduce a plant to a child. Many of the nicknames and proper names originate from the physical characteristics of the plants. Of the many legends associated with the common blue violet, the following two myths come from Katherine M. Beal's book *Flower Lore and Legend.* These are just two of many origin myths associated with the genus *Viola.*

Midas, the King of Phrygia, had a beautiful daughter called Ianthis, who was betrothed to Atys. Apollo chanced upon her one day and was so taken by her beauty that he demanded Ianthis in marriage. Her father hated Apollo and refused to allow her to break off her engagement to Atys. Apollo made up his mind to carry her off as Pluto did Proserpina. A handmaiden of the Goddess of Love Diana, Ianthis cried out to her for help when the wicked sun-god seized her from his chariot. Diana heard her handmaiden's anguished cry and changed her into a wild blue violet. Hidden from sight, by her own green leaves, Apollo was forced to leave without her. Since then, according to legend, "The violets have blossomed in the shade, which their own leaves have made."

Johnny-jump -ups or heartsease have always been associated with unrequited love and fairies; this fun tidbit of flower lore explains how it all came about. Once upon a time, some very foolish little sprites fell in love with some handsome youths whom they met during one of their visits to earth. They were young and did not realize that "fairies cannot with mortals mate". When their Queen heard of this, she was very angry and forbade them ever to leave Fairyland again. The poor little things were so grieved that they wasted away and died. Cupid felt so sorry for the lovelorn sprites that he persuaded the Fairy Queen to change them into a flower called heartsease. Ever since, these dear little plants have been associated with a broken heart.

Playing With Violas

Children have used pansy flowers as the faces of ephemeral dolls, laying the flowers across the ground and dressing them up in leaves and other plant materials. According to German and Scottish folktales, pansies were called stepmother; the large colorful lower petal is the stepmother. The two large petals to either side are her two well-dressed daughters. The two upper petals are her plainly dressed stepdaughters. If you turn the flower over, you will see the five sepals, which represent chairs. The stepmother has two chairs, while her daughters each have a chair to sit on, and sadly her two stepdaughters must share one chair.

Violet Roosters is a flower game that children have played with wild violets dating back centuries. Children would divide into two teams. Each team collected an equal number of long-stemmed violets and sat down facing each other. Each player would take a violet in hand and hook the head of the violet flower under the head of his opponent's flower. The projecting spur under the curved stem at the base of the violet worked like a hook, interlacing the two flower heads together. The children would pull until the stronger conquered the weaker by popping off the head of their opponent's flower. Whichever team accumulated the most flower heads won the game.

In her book *Child Life In Colonial Days* published in 1888, author and historian Alice Morse Earle describes playing with "quaint, antique-shaped boats with swelling lantern sail and pennant of striped grass made from the flat sword-like leaves of the flower de-luce! Filled with flowers, these leafy boats could be set gayly adrift down a tiny brook in a meadow, or with equal sentiment, …the purling gutter of a hillside street. The flowers chosen to sail these tiny crafts were the most human of all flowers, pansies, or their smaller garden sisters, the ladies delight, Johnny-jump-ups, that turned their happy faces to us from every nook and cranny of the garden."

Flower Juice Painting

Materials Needed
- Colorful fresh flower blossoms and fragrant herb leaves
- Absorbent paper
- Good imagination

Collect whole flower heads and herb leaves in the morning after the dew has dried. Pansies, violets, dianthus, zinnias, and salvia all produce bright, vivid colors. Fragrant leaves of scented geraniums, sage, lavender, and mint give lovely shades of green.

A porous paper works best for this project. Use the flower blossoms the same way you would use small sponges or paint brushes to add soft pastel colors to pencil drawings or create colorful free-form paintings. Children and adults both enjoy this natural, plant-based coloring project.

Violet Chemistry

Chemists and amateurs alike once used the juice from mashed violet flowers to determine the acid or alkaline nature of a substance. When violet flower juice is touched by an acid such as distilled white vinegar or lemon juice, the fluid turns pinkish red; if touched by an alkaline base such as ammonia or baking soda, it turns green. Children love experimenting with kitchen

Pansies come in a variety of colors. *Susan Belsinger*

chemistry; this simple recipe will visually demonstrate the color change when an acid is combined with the juice of violets, plus they can taste the change too!

Magical Lemonade with Violet Syrup

Violet syrup

Quart canning jar sterilized
2 cups fresh, pesticide-free wild blue violet flowers, calyxes and stems removed
2 cups sugar
2 cups water

Combine all the ingredients in a medium-sized pan and bring to a soft boil. Simmer for 5 minutes, stirring occasionally. Remove from heat and let cool thoroughly. Let sit for 24 hours. Strain violets from the sugar syrup into sterile jar. Store in refrigerator for up to 3 weeks.

Lemonade mix

3 tablespoons violet syrup
1 cup sparkling Pellegrino mineral water
Ice cubes
2 tablespoons fresh lemon juice

Add 3 tablespoons of violet syrup to one cup of sparkling water and stir well, then add several ice cubes. Add the 2 tablespoon of lemon juice to the water and violet syrup and stir. Then watch and savor the magic!

Petal Pulling Pansy Predictions

Pick a petal of a pansy and look at its markings:
– Four lines are a sign of hope.
– Five lines from a center branch are hope founded in fear.
– Thick lines bent to the right mean prosperity.
– Thick lines bent to the left mean trouble ahead.
– Seven streaks mean constancy in love (and if the center streak is the longest, Sunday would be the wedding day).
– Eight means fickleness.
– Nine means a changing heart.
– Eleven is disappointment in love and an early grave.

A Violet Lullaby From the 1800s

If bluebirds bloomed like flowers in a row,
and never could make a sound,
How in the world would the daisies and violets know
when to come out of the ground?

Nature teaches many lessons about diversity and learning to live together. Science helps us investigate questions. Stories and poems help us explore with our imaginations. Isn't it amazing what a *Viola* can do?

The world is but a canvas to the imagination.
Henry David Thoreau

References

Beals, Katherine. *Flower Lore and Legend.* H. Holland and Co., 1917.

Chesanow, Jeanne R. *Honeysuckle Sipping: The Plant Lore of Childhood.* Maine: Down East Books, 1987.

Earle, Alice Morse. *Child Life in Colonial Days.* Berkshire House Publishers, 1993. (1899).

Fox, Frances Margaret. *Flowers and Their Travels.* Bobbs-Merrill Company, 1936.

Lovejoy, Sharon. *Hollyhock Days.* Interweave Press, 1991.

Susan Betz has been actively involved in growing and using herbs to educate the public about gardening and the natural world for over 40 years. She is an Honorary Master Gardener, a member of the International Herb Association, Garden Communicators, National Gardening Bureau, and the Ecological Landscape Alliance. Susan is a life member of the Herb Society of America. She is the author of *Magical Moons & Seasonal Circles: Stepping into the Circle of the Seasons; Neighboring with Nature: Native Herbs for Pleasure and Purpose,* and *Herbal Houseplants: Grow Beautiful Herbs Indoors: For Flavor, Fragrance and Fun.*

Confederate violets, *Viola sororia* forma *priceana*, foreground;
V. sororia 'Freckles' in back. *Susan Belsinger*

Growing Violets from Seed

Theresa Mieseler

Bouquet of violets

Writing about violets brought back memories of when I was a child. I was raised on a dairy farm, and we had property with woods and a creek running through it. In early spring my siblings and I would forage through the woods gathering wild phlox, columbine, merrybells, meadow rue, and violets. The fragrant flowers never lasted long but Mom always showed her loving appreciation for our little bouquets.

The many colorful cultivated varieties of violets that we grow are really the offspring of violets that were found in the wild. Throughout the world, especially in Europe and Asia, there are many wild violets, and more importantly you will find them in every one of our states in the United States. Here in Minnesota, we find them in shady moist areas but also in drier sunnier spots. They are widely adaptable.

Most violets are soft-stemmed and can be perennial or annual. Globally, in Europe, woody-stemmed plants can be found; in the Andes Mountains, the longest continental mountain range in the world, along the western edge of South America, violets grow there that are completely different, with a succulent rosette form. The shape of violet leaves varies and can be round, ovate, heart-shaped, lobed, divided, or kidney-shaped—these shapes help to identify the plants, along with their location, flower color, and growth habit. Another key is that they can also be stemless, growing from the center of the top of the root, in contrast to the stemmed violets, that grow from a central stem. The distribution of the seed pods is interesting in that when fully ripened, the capsules split, and the seeds are hurled into the air to produce new seedlings. There are literally thousands of species of *Viola* to grow in home gardens.

Colorful and interesting varieties can be grown from seed with new colors and forms constantly available. It depends on the growing season, but it is usually best to sow seed indoors, approximately 8 weeks before planting in the ground or containers.

It is easy to germinate violets from seed to grow new varieties. Seeds purchased from a nursery will be true to form. If you collect seed from your own plants, they can perhaps vary, and may not be true to the parents if several varieties of violets were grown together. Purchased seed is reliable from commercial sources, with a wide range of shapes, flowers, and fragrances available. In cold weather regions, seed should be sown in late winter or spring so that there is time to reach maturity in order to survive the winter.

Violet seedlings

When sowing seed, use a sterile, soilless medium to fill your pots or seed trays. Sprinkle the seed over the top of the mix—avoid sowing the seeds too thickly. Cover the seed sparsely with the same sowing mix, making sure not to cover too thickly. Chances are that the seeds will not germinate if they are covered too deeply. I have even sowed seeds and not covered them at all with mix—just keep the surface moist and cover with light poly or even food wrap. To keep the medium moist, spray with a mist bottle so as not to scatter the seed. It is advisable to do this step of the process indoors to avoid heavy rains, winds, and other weather conditions. *Viola* seed does not require bottom heat and prefers a temperature range of 62° to 68°F. Sun or supplemental light is not necessary for germination.

Within two weeks the seed will begin to germinate, and at this point it is essential to move to sunlight and provide air movement with a small fan to avoid damping off. Within ten to fourteen days, the seedlings can be carefully lifted and transplanted to individual containers, planting them to the depth of the cotyledons, the first pair of true leaves. *Viola* roots are very tender at this stage and need to be carefully taken out of the seedling container to avoid root damage. When plants have matured and weather permits, transplant into the garden or containers. Enjoy your violets!

These are recommended sources to purchase seeds:
The Whole Seed Catalog www.rareseeds.com
Thompson Morgan Seeds www.thompson-morgan.com/seeds
Select Seeds and Plants www.selectseeds.com

Art and photo from www.Shutterstock.com.

Theresa Mieseler and husband, Jim, founded Shady Acres Herb Farm in 1977, where they grew both common and unique herbs plus vegetables—heirlooms were a specialty. Theresa is a lifetime member of the Herb Society of America, and in 2010 was awarded the Nancy Putnam Howard Award for Excellence in Horticulture. As an International Herb Association member, Theresa served as vice-president and board member. In 1999 Theresa introduced 'Shady Acres' Rosemary. As of 2016, they no longer grow plants for sale. Since then, Shady Acres Herb Farm has been moving in a different direction; now the focus is teaching others about growing plants, through Theresa's monthly newsletter, presentations, and events. Visit them at www.shadyacres.com. In March 2019, Theresa's book, *Beyond Rosemary, Basil, and Thyme,* was self-published.

Violets Seeded in Summer for Fall Blooms
By Deb Jolly and Tina Marie Wilcox

It was a cold work day at the Ozark Folk Center State Park in Mountain View, Arkansas, in early January of 2021. We were in the greenhouse, planning the timing of our seed sowing projects. We had already decided that we would grow as many *Viola* seed varieties as we could get to preview *Viola: Herb of the Year 2022* for the Heritage Herb Garden, preparing for both the 2021 and 2022 season.

In late February, we planted many flats of viola varieties under pink LED grow lights in the greenhouse—being sure to save some seeds of each variety for sowing later.

As soon as the their first true leaves appeared, the violas were placed outside in the cold to mature naturally. The flats were brought inside a cold frame during hard freezes below 28°F to avoid freeze burn on the leaves.

In late March throughout April, violas were transplanted around the gardens and in decorative pots.

Then, as expected, these cool season annuals died as the summer heated up.

The Challenge to Fool Mother Nature

We had reserved samples of the viola seeds to plant later in the season because the 2021 International Herb Association Conference was to be held at the park in late October.

IHA conferences always showcase the upcoming Herb of the Year™. Our determined mission was to time the summer viola seed planting so that these spring-blooming plants would somehow, magically, be in full flower for this auspicious event.

With the information on the seed packages and a calendar we ciphered out that we had to sow the seeds in early August to give them enough growing time to be in glorious bloom by October 30. On average, our *Violas* would begin flowering between 12 to 14 weeks after germination.

Now mind you, we were experienced, observant gardeners.

We knew good and well that our viola seeds were cool season annuals. Except for perennial blue violets, *V. sororia*, nary a species of *Viola* had ever, between the months of July and September, been spotted growing for money or for free in the Arkansas Ozarks.

When gardening in winter, we spied and spared the emerging seedlings of wild Johnny-jump-ups, *Viola rafinesquii;* then, come March, we would admire and then nibble the diminutive flowers. We observed that they like it cool to germinate, cold to grow and cool to flower and set seed.

Between us, over decades, we had purchased nursery stock and planted literally hundreds of pansy and viola bedding plants for fall, mild winter and spring flowers in the landscape and in the kitchen.

We both planted *Viola* seeds in late winter plenty of times. The quandary was, could we even get the seeds to germinate in hot germination medium and then trick the developing plants into growing like it was February/March and not August/September?

We then suddenly realized that since big growers produce *Viola* crops for fall and winter sales, we could figure out how to fool Mother Nature too.

A Google search produced an article from the online trade magazine, *Greenhouse Production News* at https://gpnmag.com/article/cool-temps-and-bright-light-treat-pansies-right-0/. After reading "Cool Temps and Bright Light Treat Pansies Right" by James E. Faust and Kelly P. Lewis we understood how annual *Violas* process light and temperature.

When temperatures are above 80ºF and the daylight is 14 hours long, *Violas* don't waste time setting down roots. They bolt. The leaves and flower buds grow fast, in a race to produce seeds before heat brings death. This is the natural *Viola* response to the long light hours and high temps. The roots cannot keep up with the tops. Root rot from overwatering results in disease. Not watering enough stunts growth. It's not easy to fool Mother Nature.

Big growers use plant growth regulators, fungicides and insecticides to bring summer-sown violas to market in the fall. We were not interested in applying chemicals to our *Violas*. Instead, we applied our intellect.

We needed to grow the seedlings in an environment not to exceed a daily 24-hour average of 80°F and, just as important, provide full sun. The average Arkansas August temperature was +84ºF.

The solution was to achieve the average temperature requirement. We left the violas outside for about six hours of sun during the day and then brought them into the air-conditioned Herb Shop, placing them on the cold cement floor to chill and rest.

The average daytime temperature in August was +93°F.

The Herb Shop's cement floor and air conditioning were the perfect conditions for germinating the seed and cooling the plants to achieve the average temperature.

How Our *Viola* Seeds Were Sown & Grown

These were the *Viola* varieties we selected to sow and show for the 2021 International Herb Association Conference.

We moistened the potting medium before planting the seeds.

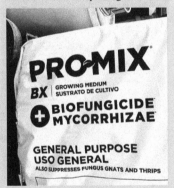 

Since *Viola* seeds are tiny, pelleted seeds were easier to sow.

Pelleted (coated)   non-pelleted

The seeds were gently and thoroughly watered into the medium.

We needed to keep the medium below 65°F to germinate the seeds—not a problem on the cold cement floor.

The seed flats were covered with plastic domes to retain moisture, humidity and temperature.

Plastic trash bags protected the floor.

Although estimated germination was listed as 14 to 21 days, the first seeds emerged in seven days.

Once a seedling popped, the dome was removed.

As the seeds germinated, the flats were placed outside during the day for watering, fertilization and six hours of sunlight.

Then the seedlings were returned to the Herb Shop floor for the cool, long night.

September's cooler temps allowed the plants to remain outside 24 hours a day for extra sunlight.

The violas began to bloom in seven weeks—as planned— in plenty of time for the IHA conference.

Sweet Success!

We hope that by sharing the story of our experiment we have inspired you to sow the seeds of some of the unusual varieties that are available for these colorful and useful herbs.

Personalize your sowing schedule to achieve your vision for the cool season in your garden.

Grow *Viola: Herb of the Year 2022*!

Photo credits: Debbie Jolly, Susan Belsinger and Tina Marie Wilcox.

Deb Jolly bio on page 33
Tina Marie Wilcox bio on page 67

Yellow Forest or Downy Yellow Violet, *Viola pubescens*
Hell Creek Natural Area, Stone County, Arkansas.
Deb Jolly

The Value of Native Violets

Karen O'Brien

When beechen buds begin to swell,
And woods the blue-bird's warble know,
The yellow violet's modest bell
Peeps from the last year's leaves below.

By William Cullen Bryant
"The Yellow Violet"

Spring certainly brings wildflowers to mind, and none more so than the violet. It grows seemingly everywhere, from the forest floor to damp or moist spots, or dry, sandy soil in open sun, even to cracks in pavements where its sturdy root system makes it almost impossible to pull out. The flowers are small, usually, in relation to the leaves, but lovely to see and often bloom throughout the season. All can be easily propagated by seed, and many spread by runners, causing some to look at the plant as troublesome or weedy.

The violet is pollinator-friendly, though not as desirable as more open, circular flowers like roses or buttercups, which invite pollinators to the center where the nectar is found. The unique design of five petals, with four usually arching slightly backward and the fifth in the lower middle, causes confusion to bees and other insects, as they are lopsided and irregular. The flower is often drooping, as well, which prevents rain and dew from washing away the pollen but makes the flower less visible to insects. So, the violet has come up with a plan to lure the pollinators inside. There are delicate lines running down and into the center of the flower on the two upper leaves, sort of a runway guide to its center where the nectar and pollen await. These lines are known as "honey guides" and show the pollinator the way to the goodies. There are also fine, soft hairs inside the flower which are a deterrent to ants and other small crawlers who might steal the nectar and pollen. These tiny insects are too small to create the shaking of the stamens which would be necessary to ensure proper pollination. The violet has again figured a way to benefit itself and guarantee that it will survive.

The droop of the flowers caused an old French botanist to suggest that the flower was pondering on its stalk. He called it "pensée" or thought, which eventually derived into "pansy." As Shakespeare wrote in Hamlet: "There's pansies, that's for thoughts."

Our Native Violets

There are hundreds of violas around the world, with over 75 species found north of Mexico. They hybridize freely, so many variants may be found. The flowers can be blue, purple, white, and even yellow. I had a magenta one in my prior garden—it was very striking and most prolific. Too bad I never thought of bringing some to my new home. It was a bit of a thug, but I miss its bright color and rampant nature.

The violets that are native to North America are spread far and wide. Most are between 6 to 10" tall, but there are some very small and some larger varieties. Here are some of the more common ones, grouped by color of flowers.

White

Viola canadensis – Canada violet – white veined with purple – heart-shaped leaves, blooms even into November is some areas

Viola blanda – Sweet white violet – light brown or purple veins – the only truly fragrant native, one of the first wildflowers to bloom

Viola pallens – Northern white volet – similar to *blanda,* but only slightly fragrant, lacks reddish coloring on the scapes

Viola primulifolia – Primrose leaved violet – leaves shaped like primrose, white flowers with purple veins on lower petals

Purple

Viola sororia – Wooly blue – this is one of the most common violets with large, showy flowers, but tends to be aggressive

Viola rostrata – Long-spurred violet – violet with dark centers, 1/2" long spurs

Viola canina – Dog violet – heart-shaped leaves, pale violet flowers

Viola septemloba – Southern coast violet – mature leaves deeply lobed; found in southern sandy pinelands

Viola adunca –Western dog violet – hairy, compact plant; native to western meadows and forests

Blue

Viola palmata – Common blue violet – heart-shaped leaves, flowers from pale blue to purple, lower petal spurred at base

Viola pedata – Birds foot violet – finely divided leaves, deep blue flowers, large and velvety – one of the prettiest violets

Viola cucullata – Blue marsh violet – long-stemmed violet of the swamps

Viola consperso – also known as Dog violet – likes boggy woodlands, often disappears in summer

Yellow

Viola pubescens – Downy yellow violet – broad, heart-shaped toothed leaves covered with whitish down underneath, yellow flowers veined with purple

Viola rotundifolia – Round-leaved violet – large, flat, shiny leaves – tiny yellow flowers borne singly on low scape, can often be found with snow still on the ground

Viola eriocarpa – Smooth yellow violet – similar to *V. pubescens,* but grows in moister areas

Viola hastata – Halberd-leaved violet – distinct oblong, heart-shaped leaves, very small yellow flowers

Bi-color or color variations

Viola papilinacea – Butterfly violet – strong growing and persistent, large flowers vary from deep blue to white – makes a great ground cover

Viola rafinesquei – Johnny-jump-up – not to be confused with *Viola tricolor,* this western native sports whitish or yellow flowers, or purple flowers with a yellow eye

Viola pedata bicolor – Two-colored birds foot violet – delicate and showy, with finely cut leaves, upper flowers a rich purple, the lower pale blue; one of the showiest of violets

Native Uses for Native Violets

Native people used violets for both food and medicine. Scientists have learned that violets produce a chemical similar to aspirin. They are also rich in rutin, which strengthens capillary walls. There is as much as 200 to 2300 mg in just a half cup of fresh violet flowers. Leaves are a source of beta-iodine, which is a natural fungicide, so they may have some effect on wounds. Nutritionally, violets also have large amounts of Vitamins A and C. Native people relished both the leaves and flowers and ate them fresh or in soup. They also made a syrup of violets to add to their gruel, a sweet treat to be sure. A decoction of the leaves was often consumed as a before-bed drink. How did they know what the 16th century *Askhams Herbal* had written about violets?

> *For thee that may not slepe for sickness seeth this herb in water and at even let him soke well hys feete in the water to the acles, wha he goeth to bed, bind the herbe to his temple and he shall slepe wel by the grace of God.*

The Ojibwa made a decoction of the roots of white violet for bladder pain. Interestingly, the decoction of the yellow violet root was used for sore throats. The Potawatomi used the roots of the yellow violet as a tonic for heart problems, and other tribes used violets for various ailments such as diarrhea, fever, gas, headaches, or poor circulation. Violet poultices were used for headaches, and the powdered root was employed as an emetic. Violet flowers or seeds were mixed with honey as a laxative for children.

Violets have played a role in our natural history, as well as in our hearts. Who doesn't love a small bouquet of violets, lovingly picked by a child, or a jar of glistening violet jelly, its flavor so unique and evocative of the woodlands? A small flower, to be sure, and often overshadowed by showier floral cousins. But a sweet delight and a promise of more springs to come.

References

Aiken, George D. *Pioneering with Wildflowers*. Stephen Daye Press, 1946.

Cullina, William. *The New England Wild Flower Society Guide to Growing and Propagating Wildflowers*. Houghton Mifflin Co, 2000.

Densmore, Frances. *How Indians Use Wild Plants for Food, Medicine & Crafts*. Dover Publications, 1974.

Hardinge, E.M. *With the Wild Flowers–From Pussy-Willow to Thistle-Down*. New York, NY: The Baker & Taylor Co., 1894.

Kindred, Glennie. *Letting in the Wild Edges*. Permanent Publications, 2013.

Parsons, Frances Theodora. Charles Scribner's Sons, 1926.

Rickett, H.W. *Wild Flowers of America*. Crown Publishers, 1987.

Scully, Virginia. *A Treasury of American Indian Herbs*. Bonanza Books, 1970.

Shimer, Porter. *Healing Secrets of the Native Americans*. Black Dog & Leventhal Publishers, 2004.

Tozer, Frank. *The Uses of Wild Plants*. Green Man Publishing, 2007.

Karen O'Brien's herbal business "The Green Woman's Garden" www.greenwomansgarden.com is located in the town of Richmond, NH and she is now gardening in the woods, as well as the fields. She has unusual herb plants, including medicinal and native herbs, for sale, runs workshops on various herbal adventures, and participates at farmers markets and fairs. Karen lectures and presents workshops on all aspects of herbs and gardening. A Master Gardener and UNH Coverts Coordinator, she was the Northeast District Member Delegate for The Herb Society of America, the Botany and Horticulture Chair of HSA, past Chair of The New England Unit of HSA, was past Secretary of the International Herb Association, and is Past President of the Greenleaf Garden Club of Milford, MA. She is the editor and contributing author to several Herb of the Year™ books, including *Capsicum*, *Savory*, *Artemisia*, and *Elderberry*, produced by IHA. Karen also writes a gardening column for the Richmond Rooster, and is the secretary for the Agriculture Commission for Richmond.

Pansies come in violescent hues. *Susan Belsinger*

Viola and Me

Chuck Voigt

My maternal grandmother Irma Jolly died when I was about one year old, so I can't say that I ever knew her, although she probably held me and did the things a grandma does with her daughter's fourth baby. I was probably bounced, cuddled, and kissed by her.

One of my first horticultural memories is tied to her death. When I was three or four, Mom and I went to Tony Panozzo's produce, greenhouse, and florist shop on the west side of Kankakee, Illinois, to buy flowers to plant on Grandma's grave. I doubt I felt the loss of her at all, being too young to have known about hers, or any death, for that matter. It was just my first remembered experience of the wonderful sights and smells of a greenhouse in spring. Looking back, I realize that my memory happened within two or three years of my mother's losing her mother to an ugly abdominal cancer, so the grief must still have been acute for Mom.

At any rate, that day I remember Mom buying flowers for the grave, which may have included double petunias and other pretty species, but what sticks with me after almost seventy years is the sense memory of the subtle, warm, and sweet fragrance of the pansies that we bought that day. They were likely 'Swiss Giant Hybrid', or some similar cultivar available in the early 50s. I can see the "faces" in those flowers, that ranged from white, to yellow, to blue, to maroon, and to almost blackish-purple. Now, whenever I see and smell pansies, it's "Decoration Day" and I'm back at Maple Grove Cemetery, north of my hometown of Bonfield, watching my mother lovingly planting those doomed flowers on that glacial sand dune where the graveyard was located, at the end of May, probably two months later than these cool season flowers should go into the ground here in USDA Zone 5.

Mom's favorite color was green, followed closely by purple, so when I was in Europe on a college choir tour, I bought her a little change purse decorated with purple pansies with green leaves. It was a big hit, although I believe it was probably "too pretty" for her to ever have used regularly. It was enough for me to see the fleeting joy in her eyes when she first saw it. If we ever get to the bottom of the piles of stuff in that farmhouse which was saved for "later," I suspect we'll find that purse in a special place. I don't know, but suspect, that Grandma Irma's favorite colors may also have been green and purple, which she then passed on to her ninth child, who similarly passed it on to me.

Flower breeders have been working with pansies over the years, trying to improve them. They might make the flowers larger, the colors more diverse or intense, the plants more heat tolerant or winter hardy, or for some inexplicable reason, create pansy flowers without faces. As a horticulturist, I guess I can appreciate the usefulness of single-color selections of flowers for beds and borders, but I have to admit that I can't abide a faceless pansy. It just isn't right, like breeding the stripes off a zebra, shortening the neck of a giraffe, or smoothing out the wrinkles on an elephant's trunk.

An herbal friend, Ben Miller, was showing me some of the plants on his farm near Bluford, Illinois, with his wife, Marilyn. We got to a flat of pansies and he picked one flower, held it up, and said, "It looks just like "Yo – se – mite Sam." Yes, he said it like that, not "Yo – sem - i – tee," as most of us do, but I found it very charming, and now cannot look at a true pansy without seeing the face of that little cantankerous cartoon character. Look him up and see if his outline, including the flowing mustache, doesn't scream "pansy". The cartoonist who first drew him had to have a pansy flower in mind, along with a wicked sense of irony, because Sam was anything but pansy-like, with his two six-guns loaded and ready to fire at the slightest provocation. "Reach for the sky, sidewinder!"

Along those same herbal lines, there are the violas, *Viola tricolor*, called Come and Cuddle Me, Heartsease, or, as I first knew them, Johnny jump-ups. The old-style ones look much like miniature pansies, purple with yellow and white faces. They are much hardier than the hybrid pansies, and easily self-sow, coming back year after year, unless crowded out by more aggressive herbage.

Late in the 1950s or early 1960s we brought home some of these violas, culled from Aunt Bernice's garden. (Yes, I had an Aunt Bee, years before Opie and Andy in Mayberry.) This was a little later in my horticultural life than the pansy planting at the graveyard, and these miniature violas happily self-re-seeded for many years. These were slightly different than the most common ones, in that they didn't have the yellow and white down in the face but were solid dark purple. The face was less distinct, black on purple, but still there, with a few radiating lines of darker color.

My first acquaintance with the name "heartsease" was when I met Sharon Lovejoy around 1993, listening to her lecture at the IHGMA conference in Seattle, and seeing her slides of the namesake of her herbal business, Heartsease. This opened the whole herbal medicine concept of these plants being effective in maintaining a healthy heart. While I do not know if they have helped my heart in that direct fashion when I have consumed them, I do know that these happy little flowers seldom fail to bring a big smile to my face and an easing of whatever tensions may be lurking within me.

The most intrepid ones I have ever seen were at Buffalo Springs Herb Farm, near Raphine, Virginia, at the restored colonial home of Don Haynie and Tom Hamlin, in the mid-1990s. There, the sprightly little Johnny jump-ups had self-sown around the patio beds, in between the paving stones, and even in the mortar between the bricks on the chimney, up to eye level or higher (5 to 6 feet). The seed capsules burst and eject the seeds with some force, so I can see how the seeds got there—just not how the plants survived and grew to flower in a medium as inhospitable as mortar! Their only concession was to grow slightly shorter the higher up they landed, probably due to a shortage of moisture.

Then there are violets themselves. I never knew our farm without carpets of violets, but my two oldest siblings, Norma and Roger, apparently introduced them from the garden of their piano teacher. With their shovels and tin cans, they brought in these pioneer violets, which quickly moved about the several acres the great-grandparents had populated with a variety of trees. Most likely these are *Viola sororia*, the common blue violet, which is the state flower of Illinois, although I just visited a website talking about the violet being the Illinois state flower, which featured only pictures of pansies. Fortunately, there are many others with the correct nomenclature and photos.

A mile west of the home place, Dad farmed the "West Place," a cleverly named 120 acres of fields and pasture. There, where the soil pH was particularly high, the color of the native violets changed to mauve, rather than the truer blue-violet of those at home. In Bonfield, on the sand hills, another violet abounded, this one a pale flat blue in color. I introduced them to the farm, with some transplanted strawberries, and they maintained that color for many years, but now seem to have been overcome by the darker blue-violet ones.

During a plant collecting spree for a plant taxonomy class in college, I collected white violets, *Viola canadensis*, from Bonfield. These are unique in that they develop aboveground stems that elongate them to a foot or more in height as the season progresses, while the others stay as ground-hugging

Bouquet of wild, common blue violets, *Viola sororia. Susan Belsinger*

rosettes. These have gained a foothold at the farm now, and still abound in and around the wooded sections of Bonfield village.

Alongside the road ditch at the West Place, I also collected one with deeply and sharply lobed leaves, which I labeled in the collection as *Viola pedata*, the birdsfoot violet. My T.A. assured me that I was mistaken, and they were not that species, but that they might possibly be a horticultural selection of regular violets, even though they were growing wild, far from any habitation. Sadly, these lived where I planted them for several years, but disappeared as other things overwhelmed them. I recently went back to the ditch bank to look for them, but they seem to have disappeared there, too, due to more rigorous mowing which encouraged aggressive grasses like tall fescue to predominate there. Also, all trees have been removed along that section of roadway, as well as the fences themselves, to allow fencerow to fencerow cultivation of the ground. Now that I am retired, I wish I'd taken better care to nurture this enigmatic plant, whether wild or horticultural. Please tell me if you've seen it elsewhere.

Among the short list of things that I could do to bring a smile to Mom's face, picking a fistful of violets, once they developed stems long enough to reach the water in a small vase, ranked high up on this list. We're not talking five or ten stems, but a nice nosegay of fifty or more. Usually, at least once a year, I would play this trump card, no matter how tedious the process. After all, I was the kid who once picked up over a bushel of acorns when they offered me a penny per pork and bean can-full, to get them out of the way (and possibly to get me out from underfoot). They soon realized their mistake and revoked the offer after the first bushel, which I think they fed to the pigs.

People who have bought into the whole sales pitch of the lawn care industry look for ways to control violets in their grassy yards. If that's their mindset, more power to them. I, on the other hand, put off mowing several large areas on the farmstead, just to enjoy the carpet of color that violets provide, for a couple of months each spring. Then I reluctantly buzz them off, about the time the foliage of snowdrops, scilla, and snow glories is dying down, so that all the taller weedy stuff gets cleared away for the rest of the season. The violets don't seem to mind very much, and come back again, year after year.

As a final anecdote, I'll mention Viola Wenzelman Meyer, a lady in our church, approximately the age of my folks. Whenever Mom was peeved with Dad, she would invoke Viola's name as his former "girlfriend," even though no serious relationship ever existed, I don't believe. In any event, she was the first, and possibly the only, person named Viola I have ever known. I will remember her as we celebrate genus *Viola* as Herb of the Year.

Charles Voigt is a retired faculty member at the University of Illinois at Urbana-Champaign. He was a state vegetable and herb specialist there from 1988 through 2015. In 1989, he was on the steering committee that wrote the bylaws forming the Illinois Herb Association. He first presented a talk at the International Herb Growers and Marketers Association (later renamed International Herb Association or IHA) in 1991. He was head of the host committee for IHA's 1995 conference in Chicago, IL, and again in 2010 for the conference in Collinsville, IL. At the Portland, OR, IHA conference in 2001 he received IHA's Service award, and in 2010, in Collinsville, IL, their Professional Award. In 2014 in Toronto, he presented the Otto Richter Memorial Lecture at the annual IHA conference. He served on the IHA Program Committee for many years and has been the chair of the Horticulture Committee since 1997. This committee has been instrumental in choosing and promoting Herbs of the Year. Chuck is currently the chair of the IHA Foundation, as well. He also wrote the popular book, *Vegetable Gardening in the Midwest*, with his vegetable mentor, Dr. Joseph Vandemark. One of Chuck's goals in retirement is to sing in 100 gardens, although the current pandemic has put a crimp in that process and he's stalled at seventeen.

whiskered pansy face
what a delight to behold
joyous harbinger

Susan Belsinger

Whiskered pansy faces. *Susan Belsinger*

Tiny *Viola rafinesquei* often grow wild in lawns and fields. *Susan Belsinger*

Gardening with Volunteer Violets

Tina Marie Wilcox

In the Arkansas Ozarks, in early springtime, all over the land, freely and exuberantly, the season is heralded in with great swaths of pastel colors. Cold souls awaken; sap and insects rise up from the warming soil. Gardeners emerge from houses and walk about, stretching out seated stiffness and begin the ephemeral appreciation for what is simply growing.

In untilled gardens, fields, and meadows, amongst the pink and purple tubular henbit and deadnettle flowers, those with an eye for detail will spy the tiny painted faces of annual Johnny-jump-ups, *Viola refinesquei*. (This *Viola*'s other common name is the North American field pansy, not to be confused with *V. tricolor*, the European wild pansy, which is also known as Johnny-jump-up.)

These charming flowers are *chasmogamous*. This romantic word means that the blooms openly display their sexual parts to actively attract pollinators to promote cross pollination. As summer comes on, these dimorphic violets will transition to the production of *cleistogamous* flowers that are only visible to the botanically curious. During this phase, the flowers are borne low, under the cover of leaves. Botanists report that the sepals are tightly closed and there are few, if any, petals. The male anthers deposit pollen directly on to the stigmas, producing self-pollinated seeds inside of capsules that are kept hidden from the casual observer. Theses seeds are more numerous in number and more fertile than those produced in chasmogamous fashion, insuring the survival of the species.

This information is good to know for those who want to encourage the presence of native wildflowers in their gardens. When weeding out the spent henbit and deadnettle, spare the Johnny-jump-ups. They are harmless and small; they will reward your efforts with many more extra early flowers the next spring.

On shaded hillsides and sunny clearings, colonies of the little wood violet,

V. sororia, take hold and spread by self-sown seeds. The leaves of these herbaceous perennials die back to rhizomes for the winter and then form basal rosettes from which heart-shaped, deep green leaves and short-stemmed, deep violet flowers emerge in spring. Colonies of these plants make great groundcover, helping to retain topsoil on sloped terrain and discourage less desirable volunteers in cultivated spaces. As is attributed to the wisdom of Aristotle, "Nature abhors a vacuum." Why not let these attractive, uniformly short-statured spring bloomers remain in their rightful place in the landscape? If some rowdy clumps of violets spread too close to specimen plants in the garden, simply harvest those troublesome space invaders. The young leaves will thicken a stew while adding nutrition to the meal. The flowers may be nibbled out of hand, candied, or strewn on salads for a respectable dose of vitamin C.

These two species, the first an annual and the last a perennial, are among a host of violets that occur around the world. Violets are the sole source of larval food for the Greater Fritillary Butterfly. They can also be a part of our diets and apothecaries. As we inhabit their habitats, they are only slightly inhibited if we are educated, intentional gardeners. Those of us who learn to identify plants and their place in the greater scheme of things will deepen relationships—to the plants and to the life forms that rely upon them.

References

Clausen, Jens, et al. "VIOLA RAFINESQUII, THE ONLY MELANIUM VIOLET NATIVE TO NORTH AMERICA." *Rhodora*, vol. 66, no. 765, 1964, pp. 32–46. JSTOR, www.jstor.org/stable/23306571. Accessed 1 June 2021.

https://www.missouribotanicalgarden.org/PlantFinder/PlantFinderDetails. aspx?kempercode=m820. Accessed 1 June 2021.

Murphy, Daniel. "The Hidden Flowers of Viola". https://awkwardbotany. com/2020/07/08/the-hidden-flowers-of-viola/. Accessed 1 June 2021.

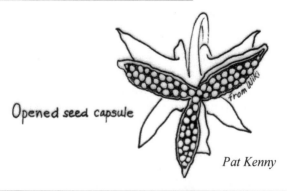

Opened seed capsule

Pat Kenny

Tina Marie Wilcox has been the head gardener and herbalist at the Ozark Folk Center's Heritage Herb Garden in Mountain View, Arkansas since 1984. She tends the gardens, plans and coordinates annual herbal events, and facilitates the production of sale plants, seeds and herbal products for the park. She is a well-seasoned herbal educator, entertainer, and, with Susan Belsinger, co-author of *the creative herbal home.*

Tina currently serves as president of the International Herb Association. She is a member of the Herb Society of America-Ozark Unit and was awarded the Nancy Putnam Excellence in Horticulture Award 2017 by the Herb Society of America.

Tina's philosophy is based upon experiencing the joy of the process, perpetrating no harm, and understanding life through play with plants and people.

Cleistomagous flower buds, common blue violet. *Pat Kenny*

Viola cotyledon, most common of the Rosulate violets. Andes Mountains.
Liam and Joan McCaughey, Alpine Garden Society, Ulster Group

Volcanic Violets

Deb Jolly

Viola volcanica

When violets come to mind, most folks think of purple wild violets growing in the yard or the African violet houseplant. As we know there are hundreds of varieties.

To my surprise, there is a *Viola* species native to Chile and Argentina, found in the Andes and it is also considered a succulent. I was sent a YouTube video to watch titled "Dazzling Bastards of the High Andes: An Introduction to Andean Violets." This is from a YouTube channel by Joey Santore, "Crime Pays but Botany Doesn't".

It was close to the end of the informative and interesting video that the camera came upon the volcanic violet.

This violet forms in a dome-shaped mound of rosettes of textured leaves, reminding me of an African violet. It grows up to 2 inches tall and is about 3 1/2 inches in diameter. It is semi- succulent with hairy and scalloped margins. The flowers have 5 white petals with violet veins and a yellow throat. They bloom in late spring and early summer. The flowers and leaves are edible fresh, cooked or dried.

This violet is very difficult to keep alive outside its native habitat.

It requires bare, loose soil which is often volcanic and is grown from seed.

Viola coronifera, very rare, confined to the
area of the Andes Mountain Cerro Colo Huincul.
Liam and Joan McCaughey, Alpine Garden Society, Ulster Group

Viola columnaris, Andes Mountains.
Liam and Joan McCaughey, Alpine Garden Society, Ulster Group

References

"Viola species, Volcanic Violet." www.davesgarden.com/guides/pf/go/250163/. Accessed October 2021.

Joey Santore. "Crime Pays But Botany Doesn't." www.youtube.com/channel/UC3CBOpT2-NRvoc2ecFMDCsA. Accessed March 2021.

"Viola volcanica, Volcanic Violets." www.worldofsucculents.com/viola-volcanica/. Accessed October 2021.

"Plant of the Month: Rosulate Violets." Liam and Joan McCaughey, August 2006. www.alpinegarden-ulster.org.uk/POM/POM Rosulate%20Viola.htm. Accessed October 2021.

Deb Voigt Jolly, a naturalist and herbalist, is the Plant Arbor and Greenhouse Specialist at the Ozark Folk Center State Park in Mountain View Arkansas, where she specializes in plant propagation. She serves as Vice Chair of the Herb Society of America Ozark Unit.

These violets were so intriguing that after Deb discovered them I did some research and found that they belong to a group of *Viola* species known as the Rosulate violets, which are descendants of the very earliest members of the genus Violaceae. Scientific evidence has shown that Violaceae originated in lush tropical forests of South America toward the end the Cretaceous Era (about 75 million years ago). The Rosulate violets evolved in response to gradual but eventually radical changes in the climate and environment into the form that exists today, with a deep tap root and succulent leaves. During the rainy season they come alive, bloom, and set seed; then they become dormant and disappear except for pips and slender rhizomes. They are at home at altitudes between 3,000 and 7,000 feet in the volcanic rubble and take from 8 to 10 years to mature.

Rosulate violets have fascinated plant hunters and alpine gardeners since they were first noticed in 1937. According to an article by botanists John and Anita Watson, "Fire and Ice: Rosulate Viola Evolution Part 1: The Stage is Set," in *Rock Garden Quarterly*, Rosulate violets "Maddeningly...so far at least, have proved themselves resolutely intractable in cultivation for all but an obsessively dedicated handful of specialist plantsmen growers."

~Kathleen Connole

Wild pansy, heartsease, *Viola tricolor.* Botanical Illustration, 1827.
(*Public Domain, plantillustrations.org*)

The Pansy ~ A Very Culitvated *Viola*

Kathleen Connole

Two members of the *Viola* genus have been greatly influenced by gardeners, horticulturists, greenhouse growers, and people who just enjoy them for their beauty. The colorful blooms that we know as pansies have been hybridized from wild violas. Parma violets, descended from a variety of *Viola alba*, and much admired for their fragrance and lovely blooms, have a very long history of cultivation by humans.

The pansies of today are descendants of the wild pansy, *Viola tricolor*; they are also commonly called heartsease. *V. tricolor*'s native range was Europe, including Britain, from Scandinavia south and east to Corsica, where it could be found growing in alpine meadows and on rocky ledges. It was first described in the 1500s by German botanists Bunfels and Fuchs. At this time, it was cultivated in German gardens as an ornamental. In 1537 the common name *pansy* was first used by the Frenchman Rusellius, in its Latin form, *pensa*, "to ponder." By the late 16th century, heartsease was being grown in the Netherlands, France, and England, and by the 1600s and 1700s it had become a popular flower in Italy, Denmark, Sweden, and Poland. Botanical illustrations of the garden pansy in 1745 "show flowers neither larger nor otherwise coloured than the wild varieties of *V. tricolor*" (Wittrock).

Another ancestor of the pansy is the mountain pansy, *Viola lutea*, native to mountainous regions of Germany, Switzerland, and England. *V. lutea* was cultivated in European gardens in the 1600s, and was known for its yellow blooms, sometimes with purple, which were larger than the blooms of *V. tricolor*.

Today's pansies, *V. xwittrockiana*, are hybrids named after Viet Brecher Wittrock (1839-1914), a Swedish botanist who made a study of the genus *Viola*, titled *Viola studier*, published in two volumes, 1895-1897. Wittrock is better known for his work on algae and spermatophytes. His herbarium of

Viola cornuta hybrids, 'Halo' and 'Northern Lights'. *Gert Coleman*

specimens, collected from 1861 to 1896 in Europe, Norway, and Sweden, is at the Natural History Museum in Stockholm. A bromeliad genus, *Wittrockia*, and an algae genus, *Wittrockiella*, were also named after him.

In 1896, while he was botany professor at Uppsala University in Sweden, Wittrock wrote an extensive article in *The Gardener's Chronicle*, "A Contribution to the History of Pansies." *The Gardener's Chronicle* was a journal of gardening and horticulture published in London in the 18th and 19th centuries. In this article he asserts that "thanks to the actions of man, those numerous varieties of garden pansies have been produced, which, in their display of flowers, so vastly surpass their wild relatives."

According to Wittrock, English gardeners in the 1800s "began to pay special attention to the Pansy." Lord Gambier of Iver, Buckinghamshire, instructed his gardener, William Thompson, to select seedlings from as many wild and cultivated pansies as possible. These selections were chosen for having the largest, most beautiful flowers. They were hybrids, most often resulting from cross-pollination by insects, as the pansies of different varieties grew side by side.

Both *V. tricolor* and *V. lutea* belong to the *Viola* section *Melanium*; these species produce fertile hybrids, unlike many other *Viola* species.

By the 1830s there were hundreds of new cultivars, and pansies were a favorite flower of the English, second only to the rose. At this time horticulturists such as Joseph Paxton developed a set of standards for the perfect pansy: "The flower-stem must be of sufficient height and strength to raise the flower above the foliage… the petals… large, flat, and without notch or fringe on the edge. The colours must be clear, brilliant, and permanent. The eye should be small compared with the size of the flower." Horticultural societies offered prizes for the finest flowers.

Amateur gardeners and professional growers cultivated pansies, always looking for new and special varieties. The owners of great estates desired to have their own collection of pansies, and the prices for the most excellent examples increased greatly.

In the 1840s special horticultural societies devoted only to pansies were formed. Their criteria for a pansy to receive an award, as stated in the Wittrock article: "The flower must be circular, the petals thick, even, and velvety, and the colour either uniform, or else, but two." Such strict requirements led to many cultivars seeming to look so much alike that they became less interesting; a need for change was "obvious."

Enter a new and fresh class of pansies from France and Belgium, called the Fancy or Belgian Pansies. These had flowers with large blotches on the three lower petals. The British at first scoffed at these and called them "French rubbish." By 1860 critics were won over by a series of outstanding varieties from the French florist Miellez of Lillie. Horticulturists in northern England and Scotland began raising these new fancy pansies in large numbers.

In 1878 the Scottish Pansy Society awarded prizes for Fancy Pansies, following a new set of very specific criteria, stated by Wittrock: "Perfectly circular form; petal edges without waviness or unevenness; large blotches (so large that they almost covered the entire surface of the flower)."

Mountain Pansy, *Viola lutea*.
Botanical Illustration. 1879.
Public Domain, plantillustrations.org

However, the popularity of these pansies soon began to wane; Wittrock says that ordinary people had "shown broader views in their ideal of beauty." The newer bedding pansies and tufted pansies were the next to be favored. Bedding pansies had smaller but much more prolific blooms, a lower, more branched growth habit; as the name implies, they were especially suited for planting out in the color beds so popular during the 1800s.

The tufted pansy, which was also known by the common name viola, was a result of purposeful manipulation by James Grieve of Edinburgh. In 1863 he crossed *Viola lutea* from the highlands of Scotland with ordinary show pansies, which were various *Viola* hybrids. This pansy was more perennial, with

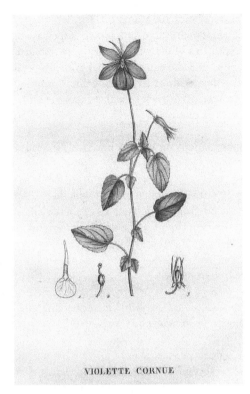

VIOLETTE CORNUE

Horned pansy, *Viola cornuta*.
Botanical Illustration. 1830.
Public Domain, plantillustrations.org

smaller, tufted flowers that were not circular. Dickson and Company, Edinburgh, crossed the fragrant horned or tufted violet, the Pyrenean *Viola cornuta*, with the dark purple garden pansy 'Vanguard' in 1867. By the late 1800s the tufted pansies were called rayless violas and the flowers were of one solid color, with no rays or streaks.

Another hybrid pansy called the Violetta was created by Dr. Charles Stuart, by crossing *V. cornuta* with 'Pansy Blue King'. This new pansy was perennial, and the almost pure white flowers were very small and fragrant.

Wittrock describes pansies of the "present day" (1898) as being "an aggregation of very different forms of plants produced by hybridization between various species of *Viola*." In his opinion *V. lutea* was a more influential ancestor than *V. tricolor*. He describes the dilemma of naming these hybrid pansies, saying that "they cannot exactly be compared to what in systematic botany is termed a species or variety... If a general Latin name seems desirable, I should propose *Viola* x*hortenses grandiflora*, when 'x' signifies the hybrid nature of the forms belonging hereto; the word 'hortenses' that they are garden plants; and the word 'grandiflora' that they are large-flowering; this to distinguish them from the small-flowering garden *Viola* of the type of *Viola odorata*." In the end, the garden pansy was named simply, *Viola* x*wittrockiana*, after Mr. Wittrock.

By 1898, when Wittrock wrote his article, the garden pansy was very different from its wild ancestors. The shape was very nearly circular; there was great variety in colors, although pure blue and pure red were rare. The dark rays of the wild relatives had been developed into the large dark blotch at the base of the three lower petals. Two characteristics of the wild pansies were retained: the "eye" was always bright yellow, and the tip of the spur was always a shade of violet. The yellow eye is important as a "honey guide," ensuring fertilization by insects seeking the nectar. Wittrock speculates that the violet color of the spur tip was to protect the nectar.

Wittrock includes several recommendations on how to improve the garden pansy:

- Develop perennial varieties by crossing garden pansies with the long-spurred violet, *Viola calcarata*, from the mountains of southeastern Europe, the Tartarian violet, *V. altaica*, from Russia, and *V. latisepala*, from the Balkan peninsula; all perennial and easy to grow.

- Produce varieties that come true from seed.

- Encourage more fragrant pansy cultivars, by using the more odiferous species *V. cornuta* and *V. lutea* var. *grandiflora*.

In closing, Wittrock states: "The garden pansies plainly prove what human intelligence, coupled with skillful perseverance, can perform in a department where it is a question of giving pleasure to millions by caring for, improving, and multiplying…forms of these lovely plants, which Nature, even in the North, so generously offers us."

It is good that credit is given to Nature in this statement, as it turns out that only certain species of *Viola* readily lend themselves to such manipulation; and even then, it was Nature that first had a hand in developing the many hybrid forms of the garden pansy.

The genus *Viola* is divided into sections, a taxonomic division between genus and species. The species from which the pansy descended all belong to the section *Melanium*. This section is unusual compared to others in the genus due to its ease of hybridization. *Violas* belonging to *Melanium* share some common characteristics that help explain this phenomenon. As Wittrock observes, no matter how human intervention changed the appearance of the pansy, they always kept the bright yellow "eye" to attract pollinators. Only one species of *Melanium* produces the cleistogamous flowers (self-pollinating), *Viola rafinesquei*, known as the field pansy or Johnny-jump-up. This species is the only one of the section that is native to North America, rather than

Europe. All other species of *Melanium* are exclusively chasmogamous, producing flowers that can be cross-pollinated.

The chasmogamous flowers in the *Melanium* section possess a distinct shape of the stigma which prevents spontaneous self-pollination, and always have the yellow honey guide spot on the lower petal, as Wittrock mentions, important for cross pollination. The pollen grains of pansies are significantly larger than in other groups in the *Viola* genus; this is thought to be a result of hybridization. Finally, the orientation of the lateral petals facilitates access by a larger range of pollinators than most members of *Viola*.

It is always such a joyful occasion to select from the many cheerful colors of the Johnny-jump-ups and pansies available at garden centers and nurseries, feed stores, even grocery stores, in the spring. Here in Arkansas we must get them as soon as they appear, so that we can enjoy their bright blooms for as long as possible before the heat of summer causes them to wither and be gone. To think that they are so closely related, and then how remarkable it is that today we have so many to choose from, is an amazing testimonial to the talents of pansy growers through all these many years, and of course, to the happy accidents encouraged by Mother Nature.

Kathleen Connole bio on page 68

Fall blooming pansies, Bull Shoals State Park Visitor Center, Arkansas.
Deb Jolly

Parma violet, *Viola odorata* var. *parmensis*. Botanical Illustration, 1898.
P*ublic Domain, plantillustrations.org*

Parma Violets ~ The Sweetest *Viola*

Kathleen Connole

Another member of the *Viola* genus with an interesting story of humans and their love of a flower is the Parma, the "Sweet Violet." Beautiful to look at with their double blooms in shades of lavender, violet and pure white, with the classic heart-shaped leaves that make a lovely bouquet, they are also deliciously fragrant. This violet is the one that was favored by such famous historical figures as Queen Victoria, Napoleon Bonaparte and his beloved Josephine.

David Glenn of Lambley Nursery in Victoria, Australia, writes a blog about his love of the Parmas. He grows a white cultivar, *Viola* 'Comte de Brazza', and says that "One flower, let alone a whole bunch, will fill a room with its fragrance."

The history of the cultivation of the fragrant violet, *Viola odorata*, dates back to ancient Rome, where it was used for cosmetics and medicine. These violets grew wild in much of Europe, including England. By the 1700s they were used in perfumes and toiletries and were grown commercially in France and the United Kingdom.

Parmas have long been thought of as a variety of *Viola odorata*, and are still listed as cultivars of that species in some current catalogs. Recent DNA analysis has provided evidence that their primary ancestor is *V. alba* subsp. *dehnhardtii*, which originated in the Mediterranean, probably from Turkey and Italy (pubmed.ncbi.nih.gov). They were first brought to Italy by the Bourbon royal family from Portugal in the early 17th century, then taken to Parma, Italy, where they became known as the Parma violet.

The earliest cultivated varieties of these sweet Parma violets came about due to the use of violet essence in the French perfumery industry in the early 1800s. Perfume made from violets required 100 pounds of flowers to make one ounce of extract. The extraction process was extremely complicated and difficult. "Violette de Parma" was a very expensive luxury that could only be

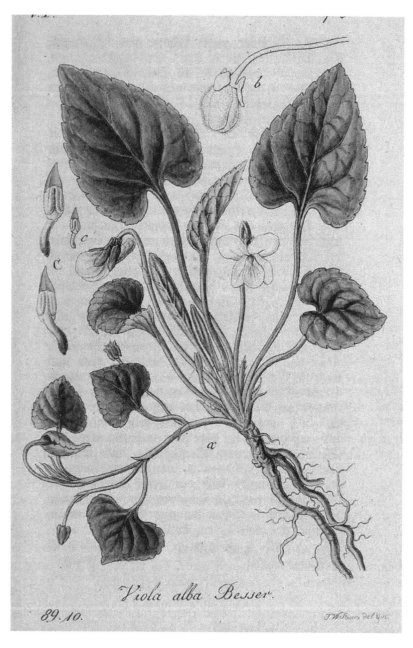

White or Parma violet, *Viola alba*, Botanical Illustration, 1845.
P*ublic Domain, plantillustrations.org*

afforded by the wealthy.

The chemistry of the scent of violets is a fascinating story of the substance *ionone*. There is a reason that although the fragrance is so sweet that it could be overpowering, it is still very alluring. After stimulating the scent receptors, ionone (from the Greek words "iona," referring to the violet scent, and "ketone," for its chemical structure) binds to them and temporarily desensitizes them. Then, after a few moments, when the scent is no longer registered, the receptors become responsive again, and the scent "pops back up" as a new stimulus, giving the brain the impression that every time a sweet violet is smelled that it is for the first time. The term for this phenomenon is *anosmia* (pubmed.ncbi.nlm.nih.gov).

There are other plants that contain naturally occurring isomeric ionones, including orris root (*Iris germanica* var. *florentina*), roses, some fruit and berries, fine Japanese green tea, and alfalfa.

The Parma violets are "morphologically well-defined cultivars… reputed for their fragrant, double flowers" (pubmed.ncbi.nih.gov). They rarely produce chasmogamous flowers, so new varieties have generally been produced from sports or mutations and then propagated vegetatively by division and stolon cuttings. Occasional cleistogamous flowers, rare in these violets, that produce a few ripe seeds could result in some genetic diversification that growers could take advantage of to produce new cultivars.

By the late 19th and early 20th centuries, when Parma violets reached their height of popularity, they were being grown in England, France, and the northeastern United States. Sir Joseph Banks is said to have cultivated 300 pots of Parmas in his glasshouses at Isleworth in 1816. According to an article at Select Seeds, "in 1874 six tons of Parmas were harvested in the south of France to supply perfumery, bouquet, and edible markets" (selectseeds.com). Much of the popularity of this very Victorian flower was due to its being a favorite of Queen Victoria; she mentioned them in her diaries over 105 times. The first entry was when she was still a princess, age 14, in 1834: "Mama gave me two very pretty little china baskets with violets and some pretty buttons." Victoria mentioned children gathering wild violets and bringing them to her during her many vacations on the French Riviera. They were grown in the flower gardens at the family retreat of Osborne, where she spent many happy days away from the pressures of being Queen of England. Today the gardens at Osborne are still being maintained, and the gardener there is working to reintroduce the flowers of Victoria, including the Parmas.

The Rhinebeck Violet Industry, postcard from early 1900s. *Public Domain*

Shipping Violets at Easter, Rhinebeck Valley, postcard from early 1900s.
Public Domain

In 1893 German chemists isolated the aroma compounds in violets and learned to produce ionones synthetically. Around this same time European commercial growers of violets for perfume were having problems due to harsh winter weather and pests destroying their crop. Economic changes in the employment market were also reducing profits. As a result, the cheaper synthetic versions of ionone began to be used in perfumes, toiletries and cosmetics, more affordable to many, but a with far less delicate fragrance.

In the state of New York, in the Hudson Valley village known as Rhinebeck, there were several very successful large-scale growers of Parma violets. There was a huge demand for these fragrant flowers in the large cities from the late 1800s into the early 1900s. In addition, practically every little home in the town had a backyard greenhouse, where the violets were grown and sold to supplement the family income. George Saltford, "Violet Specialist," published a booklet titled *How to Make Money Growing Violets* in 1902. This great little book is available as a reprint and is full of easy to understand, concise information on how to cultivate these somewhat fussy violets.

A film, "Sweet Violets: The Surprising Tale of the Violet Capital of the World – Rhinebeck, N.Y." by Tobe Carey, is an entertaining look at this story. In 2012, when the film was made, there was still one grower of fragrant violets there, Richard Battenfield. He tells of his boyhood growing up in the family business that his grandparents had begun. The theme song "Sweet Violets" is part of the fun; it will stay with you long after the film ends.

The village was also called "the Crystal City" for the glasshouses. There were over 100 households growing these violets, and it is said that "there was very little throwing of stones." One can still find shattered glass in many yards. The violet blooms were picked and bunched by workers reclining on boards across the in-ground beds. The workers then spent evening hours bundling them into bouquets, with up to 50 flowers per bunch, wrapping them and placing in shipping boxes. Women (and children during breaks from school) did this work. The boxed violets were taken to the train station in wagons to be shipped to the cities of New York, Chicago, Cleveland, Pittsburgh, Boston, Philadelphia, and Washington, D.C. Millions of blooms were shipped for holidays; the crop had to be timed to meet these key dates. The bouquets would adorn ladies' hats, gentlemen's boutonnieres, and be worn as corsages.

The cultivation of the Parma violets demanded exacting conditions in order to produce the best quality blooms. The soil and climate of the Rhinebeck seemed most favorable, with sunny days and cool nights; the violets imported to there from Europe adapted and "bloomed like never before" (Battenfield).

Most of the glasshouses were 24 by 200 feet, with the violets planted in the beds 10 inches apart. Each year after the growing and bloom season (November to April) the soil was removed and replaced with fresh new soil. The village had no indoor plumbing and many valley residents had farm livestock; their manure and the outhouse cleanings were gathered and let to sit for one year. Fresh soil from local pastures was brought in and combined with the composted manure in a ratio of 1:1 to fill the beds. Itinerant laborers would help with this work. The greenhouses were planted with new plants in mid-July. One house could hold 100,000 plants. At the end of April the plants were removed and divided; the divisions were planted in outdoor beds to be transplanted into the greenhouses in July.

During the cold New York winters the greenhouses were heated with coal; the fires would have to be stoked several times during the night. Richard Battenfield recalled that one of his chores was to soak the coal every evening so that it would burn slower. He said that then his father would get up every two hours to check the furnaces. On sunny days the vents would need to be opened as needed to maintain the cool temperatures that the violets preferred; of course, this was all done by hand. In summer the greenhouse glass was sprayed with lime to provide shade. Needless to say, this was a very labor-intensive industry, requiring much work to be done day and night during the growing and harvest season.

As fashions and tastes changed, the sweet Parma violet fell out of favor, and was replaced by other corsage flowers such as carnations and orchids. By the end of World War II violets were considered old-fashioned, the flowers of grandmothers.

When a search is done on Google for Parma violets, 9 times out of 10 what comes up will be the "Swizzels," little candies said to be "sweet with an incredibly soapy or floral taste." These were first made available in 1946; today there is nothing from violets in these candies. Such confections date back to the 1600s. They were sugary lozenges truly flavored with violets; Queen Victoria, known for her sweet tooth, was very fond of them.

Today there are a few growers working to revive these unique, beautiful sweetly-scented flowers, seeking out surviving Parma violet varieties and propagating them. Several well-known cultivars dating to the 1800s continue to be grown. Two such Parmas, 'Duchess de Parme' and 'Comte de Brazza' are offered by Select Seeds in 2.5-inch pots.

One of the most endearing qualities of the Parma violets is their inimitable sweet fragrance. Since Parmas are not easily obtained or grown, we can encourage the cultivation of other fragrant violets and pansies, such as *Viola odorata*, the wild European native, and pansy cultivars that are hybrids of *Viola cornuta*, one of the fragrant ancestor of today's pansies.

References

Combs, Roy. *Violets:The History and Cultivation of Scented Violets.* Batsford, 2013.

Coon, N., and G. Giffen. *The Complete Book of Violets.* A.S. Barnes and Company, 1997.

Glenn, David. "Parma Violets." *Garden Notes.* Lambley Nursery, Victoria, Australia. www.lambley.com.au/garden-notes/parma-violets. Accessed 2/8/21.

"How Violets and Ionones Made Perfume History." www.boisdejasmin. com/2021/05/how-violets-and-ionones-made-perfume-history-html. Accessed 10/27/21.

"In Search of Queen Victoria's Favourite Flower." www.english-heritage. org.uk/visit/inspire-me/blog/b;pg-posts/2017/in-search-of-queen-victorias-favourite-flower/. Accessed 10/26/21.

Lujain et al. "Ionone is More Than a Violet's Fragrance: A Review." *Molecules 2020.* www.pubmed.ncbi.nlm.nih.gov. Accessed 12/11/21.

Lattanzi, Edda, and Anna Scoppola. "*Viola* section *Melanium* (Violaceae) in Italy: New data on morphology of *Viola tricolor*-Group." *Webbia* 67(1):47-64, 2012. www.academia.edu/5400259/Viola_section_Melanium_Violaceae_in_Italy_New_data_on_mor-phology_of_Viola_tricolor_Group. Accessed 11/20/21.

"Origins of Parma Violets." *American Journal of Botany*, Vol. 94, Issue 1, Jan. 2007. www.pubmed.ncbr.nih.gov/216422051. Accessed 2/6/21.

Parsons, Jerry. "Pansy." *Parson's Archive, Everything Texans Ask About Gardening.* www.aggiehorticulture.tamu.edu/archives/parsons/flowers/pansies.html. Accessed 3/29/21.

Pimlico, Dan. "As Sweet as a Violet." www.candidegardening.com/GB/stories/baeba7e3-8319-4abb-966d-4ebcede84d3a. Accessed 11/16/21.

Saltford, George. *How to Make Money Growing Violets.* The Violet Culture Co., 1902.

Shinnera, Lloyd H. "VIOLA RAFINESQUII: NOMENCLATURE AND NATIVE STATUS." Rhodora, Vol. 63, No. 756, Dec. 1961. pp. 327-335.

www.jstor.org/stable/23306642. Accessed 12/30/21.

"Sweet Violets – The Surprising Tale of the Violet Capital of the World – Rhinebeck, N.Y." A film by Tobe Carey. www.vimeo.com/ondemand/sweetviolets. Accessed 3/13/21.

"Veit Brecher Wittrock." www.en.m.wikipedia.org. Accessed 10/10/2121.

Wittrock, Professor V.B. "A Contribution to the History of Pansies." *Gardener's Chronicle*, 1896. www.bulbnrose.x10.mx>Heredity/WittrockPansy1896/WittrockPansy1896/html. Accessed 10/10/21.

Kathleen Connole joined the Ozark Folk Center's Heritage Herb Garden team in 2006. Before moving to Arkansas' Buffalo River Country in 2005, Kathleen earned a degree in Plant Science from the University of Missouri-Columbia and worked at Powell Gardens and Farrand Farms in Kansas City, Missouri. She practiced plant propagation, all aspects of greenhouse growing, and artistic gardening in the designing of premier mixed containers.

Since she became the Folk Center's Horticulturist, Kathleen's passion has been to research the natural history of the Heritage Herb Garden's diverse collection of plants, both those native to the Ozarks and those from all over the world. While on hiatus due to Covid and unrelated health problems, she has continued to contribute time as a volunteer, by composing interpretive signs for the Garden and presenting programs at the 2021 Herb Harvest Fall Festival. Kathleen served as chair of the Herb Society of America Ozark Unit, headquartered at the Ozark Folk Center State Park, and currently is secretary for the International Herb Association Board and editor of the IHA's Herb of the Year™ book for 2022, *Viola*.

Pat Kenny

Sweet Violets Vintage Greeting Card. *Public Domain.*

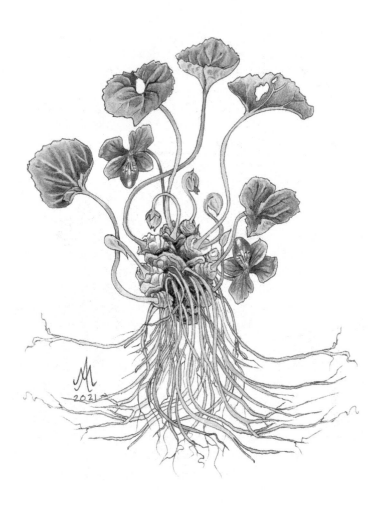

Alicia Mann

Art, Literature, & Poetry

Detail of violet with unfurling leaves. *Susan Belsinger*

Vibrant, Sensuous Violet

Gert Coleman

Immortalized in verse and prose, violets hold an estimable place in the literary canon. From ancient Greek poetry to contemporary novels, violets have been associated with springtime and early death, modesty and sensuality, the vicissitudes of love and the roles of women within society.

I love stories, especially when herbs and flowers appear in them. Plant descriptions help to depict setting or function as images and metaphors to add atmosphere and depth to plot, character, and mood. While stories can entertain, they often reveal customs, traditions, and values as well as chronicle the use of plants within cultures. *Viola*, the 2022 Herb of the Year™, has many stories to tell.

Romans placed violets on the graves of small children to commemorate innocence. Queen Victoria's gardeners grew mass quantities for posies, wreaths, garlands, candies, cordials, and remedies. Violets, roses, and primroses were strewn at weddings to symbolize modesty and purity. Dried violets scented love letters, often kept as mementos of faithfulness. Napoleon died wearing a locket filled with Josephine's violets. Violets may be placed in tussie-mussies to symbolize chastity and loyalty. Contemporary florists pair yellow roses with purple violets to commemorate a 50th Wedding Anniversary. Planted under white tulips or early roses, violets are "the most poetic of ground covers" (Fox 65).

Congenial violets work well with many flowers in gardens, arrangements, and literature. Ancient Greeks and Romans adorned statues with violets and roses in homage to Aphrodite and Venus, wore tiaras of violets and parsley to prevent inebriation, and draped lovers with violets and pansies. Unassuming little violet surprisingly symbolizes sensuality, sexual love, and hidden passions in the Greek poet Sappho's (c.630 to c.570 BCE) seductive love poems—which exist only in fragments punctuated by ellipses:

Many crowns of violets,
roses and crocuses
...together you set before more
and many scented wreaths
made from blossoms
around your soft throat...
...with pure, sweet oil
...you anointed me,
and on a soft, gentle bed...
you quenched your desire...
...no holy site...
we left uncovered...

On soft warm days, inspired by the sights and scents of the natural world, we might be tempted to feel the earth beneath our feet by going barefoot. Spring rituals have long embraced full-bodied, natural approaches to absorbing nature. In her voluptuous poem "Rolling Naked in the Morning Dew" (1998), Pattiann Rogers richly layers botanical images, including *Viola pedata*, to evoke the tactile sensuality of the arguably healthful practice of rolling naked in the morning dew:

Lillie Langtry practiced it, when weather permitted,
Lying down naked every morning in the dew,
With all of her beauty believing the single petal
Of her white skin could absorb and assume
That radiating purity of liquid and light.
And I admit to believing myself, without question,
In the magical powers of dew on the cheeks
And breasts of Lillie Langtry believing devotedly
In the magical powers of early morning dew on the skin
Of her body lolling in purple beds of bird's-foot violets,
Pink prairie mimosa.

According to folklore in Germany, Denmark, France, and Pennsylvania, swallowing the first three violets you see will protect against colds and fevers in the coming year (Arrowsmith 521). Imagine what rolling in them could do for you! Violet leaves have soothing, demulcent qualities often used in skin, urinary tract, and digestive remedies to calm irritation. This confers a softness and sensuality to violets, hidden beneath taller plants in fields and gardens.

William Shakespeare (1564–1616) reveals an affinity for plants throughout his plays and sonnets, with 160 references to herbs and flowers. Having grown up in the riverside country town of Stratford-upon-Avon, the grandson of farmers, Shakespeare was familiar with weeds, wildflowers, and cultivated plants, their scents, culinary, medicinal, and symbolic uses. Catering to the Elizabethan audience, Shakespeare scattered flowers throughout his works, partly as setting and partly as familiar icons. Two famous passages include violets working together with other flowers.

In *A Midsummer Night's Dream,* Act 2, Scene 2, Shakespeare conjures images of wildflowers to create a fantastical, almost lubricious setting where Oberon directs Puck to find Titania:

> *I know a bank where the wild thyme blows,*
> *Where oxlips and the nodding violet grows,*
> *Quite over-canopied with luscious woodbine,*
> *With sweet musk-roses, and with eglantine.*
> *There sleeps Titania sometime of the night,*
> *Lull'd in these flowers with dances and delight...*

Puck's humorous errors and mischief cause much mayhem on this romantic midsummer evening, but all ends well for the would-be lovers.

But things do not end well in *Hamlet.* Violet's association with early death—the blooms appear in early spring then fade away in summer—combines with other significant herbs to accentuate the play's sadness and dark machinations. Ophelia, the beautiful daughter of Polonius, Lord Chamberlain to the King of Denmark, has fallen in love with Prince Hamlet, the king's nephew and heir. But, brooding over his father's death and mother's treachery, he not only rejects her but murders her father as well. Bereft, Ophelia wanders through the court, passing out invisible herbs and flowers in her madness and grief (Act IV, Scene 5):

> *There's rosemary, that's for remembrance.*
> *Pray you, love, remember.*
> *And there is pansies, that's for thoughts ...*
> *There's fennel for you, and columbines.*
> *There's rue for you, and here's some for me.*
> *We may call it "herb of grace" o' Sundays.*
> *Oh, you must wear your rue with a difference.*
> *There's a daisy. I would give you some violets,*
> *But they withered all when my father died.*

Elizabethan audiences understood the symbolic language of Ophelia's flowers, more so than contemporary ones. Rosemary symbolizes sorrow and early death, while pansies allude to thoughts and memories. Ophelia hands the king a sprig of fennel, a symbol of flattery and marital infidelity; in addition, fennel flowers fade quickly, so they also suggest sadness and loss. Columbine reiterates flattery and insincerity while rue stands for regret and repentance. Daisies symbolize innocence while the violets, now withered, indicate faithfulness as well as early death. That's quite a bouquet for a court specializing in ambition, subterfuge, and treason!

In Act V, Scene 1, when Ophelia is discovered drowned, surrounded by garlands of flowers, her brother Laertes laments her loss with another reference to violets:

> *Lay her i' th' earth,*
> *And from her fair and unpolluted flesh*
> *May violets spring!*

During the Middle Ages, folks believed that the soul leaving the body could take the form of a flower. Ophelia represents the innocence of women who fall in love with the wrong person.

Like Shakespeare, the Romantic poets referenced Nature to explain and connect with inexplicable emotions. In his short poem "She Dwelt among the Untrodden Ways" (1798), William Wordsworth laments the passing of a dear friend. She lived quietly in the rural English countryside, her beauty and virtue overlooked in real life the way that violets can sometimes be:

> *A violet by*
> *a mossy stone*
> *half hidden*
> *from the eye*
> *fair as a star*
> *when only one*
> *is shining*
> *in the sky.*

Scholars have long speculated on Wordsworth's relationship to this unnamed woman, celebrated in five poems that comprise the "Lucy" series. Wordsworth compared her to both violets and stars, two positive images, but never revealed her identity.

Sir Walter Scott's much quoted poem "The Violet" (1808) also cites violet's beauty in a sylvan setting but elevates the flower to a much higher status:

> *The violet in her greenwood bower,*
> *Where birchen boughs with hazel mingle,*
> *May boast itself the fairest flower*
> *In glen, or copse, or forest dingle.*

While conventional floriography attributes Modesty and Innocence to violet, Scott's use of the words "boast" and "fairest" belies that concept, suggesting that violets have much to brag about.

Christina Georgina Rosetti uses violets and seasonality to consider the challenges of falling in love at different stages of life in "Autumn Violets" (1868). Late love begun in autumn is worth cherishing, of course, but youthful love in the spring may bloom more passionately:

> *But when the green world buds to blossoming.*
> *Keep violets for the spring, and love for youth,*
> *Love that should dwell with beauty, mirth, and hope...*

Historically, violets represent spring so strongly that, according to English folklore, violets flowering in the fall, portend a new baby in the family.

Violets have a quiet, modest beauty that takes time and effort to notice, with the flowers nodding downwards on dark, rainy, or cloudy days to prevent nectar dilution. If you have ever tried getting a close-up photograph of violet flowers, you know it can be tricky indeed. While violets may sometimes be overlooked by grownups, they are beloved by children of all ages, who love to pick handfuls. What child hasn't chanted this little rhyme?

> *Roses are red.*
> *Violets are blue,*
> *Sugar is sweet,*
> *And so are you.*

This oft-recited poem originated in Sir Edmond Spenser's *The Fairie Queene* (1590)—"Roses red and violets blew,/And all the sweetest flowers,/That in the forest grew"—but has been widely mimicked ever since. Crafting a "Roses are red" poem is a common exercise in creative writing classes. A quick internet search will reveal everything from sentimental to sarcastic to hilarious versions.

The Violet and the Crocus. Alicia Mann

As the harbinger of spring, violets seem particularly attuned to the vagaries of winter's final blasts. Cheerful flashes of early spring color, violets suggest rebirth and renewal. Unlike more delicate perennials, violets can withstand spring snowfalls and cold spells. Taught in American schools throughout the mid-twentieth century, Lenore Hetrick's poem "The Violet and the Crocus" (1937) offers two spring flowers trying to interpret the weather:

"Is it time to awaken?" the violet asked.
The crocus peeped at the sky.
"Not yet, dear flower!" she whispered low.
"Some snowflakes are going by!"
"Is it time to grow?" The violet questioned
After a day had passed.
"Not yet" said the crocus, peeping again.
"I still feel winter's blast."
The third time the violet opened her eyes,
She heard a loud, harsh sound,
It shook all the earth, the trees and the hills,
And was felt way down in the ground.
"Is it time, friend crocus?" the violet asked,
And the crocus lifted her head.
"Oh, no!" said she. "There's a wind like a lion!
It's best that we stay in bed!"
The violet opened her big, blue eyes,
"A wind like a lion, you say?
Then March is here! Wild, stormy March!
And it's time to be on our way!"

While poetry has extolled violet's beauty in natural settings, two beautifully written novels explore the social, economic, and personal effects on women in the little known business of selling fresh violets.

Hazel Gaynor's novel *A Memory of Violets: A Novel of London's Flower Sellers* (2015) depicts the intertwining lives of London women from 1876 through 1913, from the degradation of Covent Garden's fresh flower markets to the genteel warmth of upper class drawing rooms. Sweet violets (*Viola odorata*), enormously popular in the late 19th and early 20th centuries, were worn on hats, wrists, muffs, and waistbands, given as gifts, and carried to mask street odors. Violets symbolized love, innocence, and modesty.

Orphaned at an early age, two Irish sisters, Florrie, crippled, and Rose, blind, rise early in the dark before dawn to buy, tie, and fluff bunches of violets and

Close up of Confederate and common blue violets. *Susan Belsinger*

watercress. By day, they stand on busy London street corners, by night, near theaters, hawking their blooms to make a living. Florrie vigilantly watches out for little Rose while trying to make the best of it. In the month of June, she tells us, "All the sweetest flowers are in bloom this time of year, so we should have a decent trade, if the rains hold off. It's the violets and roses I like selling best. They look so pretty all tied up, and the violets with their leaves shaped like love hearts and the rose petals what feel so soft in my fingers I imagine I'm touching ladies' velvet skirts" (87).

Starving and often cold, they find strength and comfort in each other until one day tragically separated on a crowded bridge. Florrie spends the rest of her life searching for Rose, though her life improves greatly at Mr. Shaw's Training Homes for Watercress and Flower Girls, where each house is named after a flower. Here, disabled girls learn to make artificial violets, sold to decorate homes and cars or worn on lapels to commemorate Queen Alexandra. When Tilly Harper leaves the beauty and quiet of the Lake District to become assistant housemother at Violet House, their lives intersect. The scent of violets pervades the story accentuating emotions and linking characters separated by time and death.

Growing up in New York State's Hudson Valley, novelist Kathy Leonard Czepiel was stunned to learn that the area had once been known as "the Violet Capital of the World." This became the basis for her first novel, A *Violet Season* (2012): "How was it possible that I never knew this before? In fact, most evidence of that once-booming industry has disappeared" (260).

Based on exhaustive research at the Museum of Rhinebeck History and other sources, her engrossing novel examines the complicated, sometimes heartbreaking, strategies women use to survive poverty, get ahead in business, and preserve their families. During the heyday of the American violet industry, roughly the 1870s through the 1930s, farmers grew sweet-scented violets for sale from New York City up to Albany and beyond. "At the turn of the century, the valley's 400 violet houses produced six million blooms in a single growing season" (246).

According to Czepiel, "The Christmas season was always busy. Violets were part of festive decorations everywhere, and with so many parties, corsages were in demand" (105). Many homeowners see violets as an invasive lawn weed but growing violets year-round is no easy task. "I never realized how hard you had to work to grow these little flowers," a worker tells the main character Ida Fletcher on his first day planting violets in greenhouses. "I don't imagine any boy who gives them to his sweetheart has any idea" (30-31).

Women were beginning to question traditional gender roles and explore lives outside of marriage during these years. Ida, who married the black sheep, ne'er-do-well youngest brother, takes up wet-nursing to make ends meet while the rest of the Fletcher family thrives in the lucrative violet industry. Her daughter Alice is forced to leave school and find a job in the city. Told from both Ida and Alice's perspectives, intermixed with fictional interviews, this gripping story upends the concept of violet as a symbol of constancy and devotion.

Both books reveal the suffering, emotional growth, and varied experiences of women caught up in the world of violets and flowers, facing tragedy, love, and rebirth amidst the violets. No wonder these two books are so popular in contemporary book clubs!

Mirroring the rise and fall of the violet industry, floral names like Violet, Rose, Lily, Daisy, and Poppy were especially popular from the 1880s through the 1920s according to *Our Baby Namer.com*. Violet retained a steady popularity from the late 1800s through the first third of the 20th century, always in the top 100, and today is reflected in many books set during that period. For example, herbal mystery writer Susan Wittig Albert's latest series, the Darling Dahlias, depicts the lives of a dozen garden club members based in Darling, Alabama, during the 1930s. A recurring character named Violet, whose sister is named Pansy, is both beautiful and resilient, surviving the trends and downturns of the Great Depression.

Though the name Violet peaked in the 1920s, declining through the 1980s, it has begun an even higher upward trend in the United States. In the top 50 names for girls in 2020, Violet ranked 37, possibly fueled by celebrity parents Jennifer Garner and Ben Affleck. New parents may also have grown to like the name through popular television dramas set before and after World War I, like *Downton Abbey* whose character Violet Crawley, Dowager Countess of Grantham, was played by the award-winning Dame Maggie Smith. Recently, *General Hospital,* an ABC soap opera, introduced a charming, very pretty toddler named Violet to the storyline.

Conversely, characters named Violet are not always sweet or modest. The nodding flowers suggest shyness and the phrase "shrinking violet" disparages the quieter, less assertive among us. However, in literature, Violets can be anything but! The movie *Willy Wonka and the Chocolate Factory* (1971) features a brash, talkative, competitive gum chewer named Violet Beauregarde. In Lewis Carroll's *Through the Looking-Glass* (1872), Alice discovers that flowers can talk, and is taken aback when a Violet insults her: "I never saw anybody that looked stupider" (qtd in *The Literary Garden*). I'm sure you can think of many more.

Some folks see violets as a weed—many websites include advice on getting rid of this "invasive"—but whenever I bring violet plants to my herb talks or a raffle table, folks swoon over them, proclaiming a lifelong love for violets. They are often chosen from the raffle table before anything else. The past two years, I could easily find pansies but no other violas—except in catalogs, and then not many. Let's make it easy for folks to find violets. Please grow a variety of violets to celebrate *Viola* as the Herb of the Year™.

This has been my personal love song to violets, a pretty little flower and herb that deserves recognition as Herb of the Year™. Violet's beautiful purple flowers and heart-shaped leaves have won a place in our hearts and the herb garden. Violets have waxed and waned in popularity, but they have always been an integral part of culture, literature, and everyday life.

The Romantic poet William Wordsworth reminds us that, as

> *Long as there are Violets,*
> *They will have a place in story.*

Close up of 'Freckles'. *Susan Belsinger*

References

Albert, Susan Wittig. *The Darling Dahlias and the Voodoo Lily.* Persevero Press, 2020.

Arrowsmith, Nancy. *Essential Herbal Wisdom: A Complete Exploration of 50 Remarkable Herbs.* Llewellyn, 2007. 513-528.

Avia. "Symbolic Violet Meaning: A True Symbol of Love and Harmony." 8/14/2018. *What's-Your-Sign.com.* https://www.whats-your-sign.com/symbolic-violet-meaning.html. Accessed 6/10/21.

Bown, Deni. *Herbal: The Essential Guide to Herbs for Living.* Barnes & Noble, 2001. 294-298.

Candy, Melissa."Plants in Shakespeare." 4/29/2016. *Royal Botanic Gardens Kew.* https://www.kew.org/read-and-watch/plants-in-shakespeare. Accessed 9/30/21.

Coombs, Roy. E. *Violets: The History & Cultivation of Scented Violets.* 2 ed. B T Batsford, 2003.

Czepiel, Kathy Leonard. *A Violet Season.* Simon & Shuster Paperbacks, 2012.

De Bray, Lys. *Fantastic Garlands: An Anthology of Flowers and Plants from Shakespeare.* Blandford Press, 1982.

Easley, Alexis. "Love, Nature and Conquest in Macmillan's Magazine." *victorianjournalism.*10/26/2016. https://victorianjournalism.wordpress.com/2016/10/26/love-nature-and-conquest-in-macmillans/. Accessed 9/27/21.

Fox, Helen Morgenthau. *Gardening with Herbs for Flavor and Fragrance.* Dover, 1970.

Gaynor, Hazel. *A Memory of Violets: A Novel of London's Flower Sellers.* William Morrow, 2015.

Gibson, Matt. "Herbs and Flowers in Shakespeare." *Gardening Channel.* https://www.gardeningchannel.com/herbs-flowers-shakespeare/. Accessed 9/30/21.

Grieve, Mrs. M. *A Modern Herbal.* Barnes & Noble, 1996. (1931).

Hayes, Elizabeth S. *Spices and Herbs: Lore and Cookery.* Dover, 1980.

"How Popular is Violet?" *Our Baby Namer.* www.ourbabynamer.com/Violet-name-popularity.html. Accessed 9/13/21.

Kennedy, Colleen. "Smelling 'Violet' in Renaissance Works." *The Recipes Project*. 4/26/2018. https://recipes.hypotheses.org/tag/violets. Accessed 9/26/21.

King, Bernadette. "Violet: Innocence, Abundance, True Love." *BuildingBeautifulSouls.com*. https://www.buildingbeautifulsouls. com/symbols-meanings/flower-meanings-symbolism/violet-meaning-symbolism/. Accessed 4/7/21.

Literary Garden, The. Berkley, 2001.

Lust, John. *The Herb Book*. Bantam, 1974.

Nahmad, Claire. *A Wisewoman's Guide to Herbal, Astrological & Other Folk Wisdom*. Destiny Books, 1994.

P., Rebekah. "Violet Meaning and Symbolism." *Florgeous*. https://florgeous. com/violet-flower-meaning/. Accessed 4/7/21.

"Poems & Poets." *Poetry Foundation*. https://www.poetryfoundation.org/ poems.

Prager, Sarah. "Four Flowering Plants That Have Been Decidedly Queered." https://daily.jstor.org/four-flowering-plants-decidedly-queered/. Accessed 4/7/21.

Rodale's Illustrated Encyclopedia of Herbs. Eds. Kowalchik, Claire and William H. Hylton. Rodale, 1987. 498-499.

Rogers, Pattiann. "Rolling Naked in the Morning Dew." https:// orionmagazine.org/poetry/pattiann-rogers-poem/. Accessed 8/7/21.

Sanders, Jack. *The Secrets of Wildflowers: A Delightful Feast of Little-Known Facts, Folklore, and History*. Lyons Press, 2003. 48-54.

"Sweet Violet (Viola Odorata) and Parma Violet: How to Grow Forgotten Treasures." 2/14/21. *Star of Nature*. https://starofnature.org/sweet-violet-viola-odorata-parma-violet-how-to-grow/. Accessed 10/3/21.

Vanbuskirk, Sarah. "Violet Name Meaning." *Verywellfamily*. www. verywellfamily.com/violet-name-meaning-5191557. Accessed 9/13/21.

"Violet Origins and Meaning." *Baby Names DNA*. https://nameberry.com/ babyname/Violet. Accessed 9/13/21.

Waterman, Catherine H. *Flora's Lexicon*. Algrove Publ, 2001. (1860).

"What are Some 'Roses Are Red, Violets Are Blue' Jokes?" *800Flower*. https://www.800flower.ae/blog/roses-red-violets-blue-jokes/. Accessed 4/15/21.

"What do Violets symbolize in literature?" *AskingLot.com.* https://askinglot.com/what-do-violets-symbolize-in-literature. Accessed 4/17/21.

Gert Coleman loves herbs; she grows, eats, and reads avidly about them. Retired Associate Professor of English at Middlesex County College in New Jersey, she lives on 106 acres in Middlefield, New York where she and her husband are fixing up an old house, training a puppy, and planting herbs, flowers, trees, and at-risk native plants. She edited five IHA Herb of the Year™ books (*Cilantro & Coriander; Hops: Brewing and Beyond; Agastache: Anise Hyssop, Hummingbird Mints and More; Rubus;* and *Parsley*), and frequently writes about the legends, lore, and poetry of herbs. In addition, she offers zoom talks, nature walks, and nature writing workshops in wild places of New York and beyond.

magic underfoot

purple haze of violas

above green heart leaves

Susan Belsinger

Purple viola blooms float above the leaves. *Susan Belsinger*

Violette Vintage Art. *Public Domain*

The Balm of Violets: Love, Romance, & Ancient Roots

Pat Crocker

*Delicious air, made potent with benevolent herb aromas, can flow
like a balm through our thoughts and feelings...*
–Lesley Bremness, *Essential Herbs*

Who can resist any of the plants in the Violaceae family? Who doesn't ponder the heart-shaped leaves of wood violets, marsh violets, sweet violets, bog violets, or any of the estimated 500 species in this diminutive yet utterly delightful group of plants? Who hasn't felt the pull of our very heart strings when we happen to glance towards the edge of a woodland path and sense a cluster of purple or white or yellow capricious heads nodding to us in a shy, silent greeting?

Consider the Pansy, whose name comes from the French word, *penser*, to think (perhaps as Shakespeare's Ophelia offers pansies for love's sad thoughts or troubles). Another common name for *Viola tricolor* is Love-in-Idleness. *Love. In. Idleness.* Together, those words suggest that deliciously dreamy state when time slows down, and we find ourselves drifting in an expanded realm of pure bliss. And just to be sure that we get the message, some of the other curious old country names for *Viola* are Heart's Ease; Heart's Delight; Jack-Jump-Up-And-Kiss-Me; Tickle-My-Fancy; Call-Me-To-You; and Come-And-Cuddle-Me.

Eleanour Sinclair Rohde writes, "Violets preserve in their scent the memory of Orpheus, for one day, being weary, he sank to sleep on a mossy bank, and where his enchanted lute fell, there blossomed the first violet. The magic music of his lute still haunts the scent of violets."[1] And deeper into the ancient world of mythology, goddesses, and gods, we learn that two of the high priestesses of love—the Greek Aphrodite and the Roman Venus—were offered myrtle, and they were also linked to the violet along with quince, apple, and the rose.

In Shakespeare's *A Midsummer Night's Dream,* the King of the Fairies, Oberon speaks to Puck of nodding violets growing on a bank with wild thyme and oxlips. England's most famous poet also ascribes mystical, ethereal, and romantic qualities to violets with the following enchanting words from the same play.

> *Yet mark'd I where the bolt of Cupid fell:*
> *It fell upon a little western flower,*
> *Before milk-white, now purple with love's wound,*
> *And maidens call it, Love-in-idleness.*
> *Fetch me that flower; the herb I show'd thee once:*
> *The juice of it on sleeping eyelids laid*
> *Will make a man or woman madly dote*
> *Upon the next live creature that it sees.*

And if we were to pause and imagine how these humble plants got the reputation for matters of the heart, we'd have to agree with Leslie Bremness, who points out that "…ambrosial perfumes open the door to romance…"[2]. On this, science is catching up with folklore: research on fragrance at the Oxford Botanical Garden has found that humans have over a thousand primary scents that we can identify and recollect. Indeed, because unlike any other sense, our sense of smell is directly linked to our brain from our nose, and this is why it is our oldest and most primeval route to romance and passionate emotions.

In fact, love may be the balm of life, and if so, fragrance is its fuel. Even the slightest hint of violet, lavender, or rose on the wind can enliven, encourage, and expand love. Aromas have the power to connect us to the feelings or memories of our great loves. The subtle awareness of spice, honey, musk, or flowers immediately transports us to our grandparents' kitchen, or into a relationship dynamic, or the garden of a dear friend. And while the fresh, ethereal bouquet of violets, wafting, floating, or lingering on the breeze may be the first to open the secret places of your heart, it is also their precious and vulnerable paper-thin petals dancing, waving to us on demurely curled stems and luminously green, heart-shaped leaves that transport us to that state of pure, idle love. All the senses combine in violets to set them apart as universal symbols of love.

If Shakespeare was aware of the language of flowers, and many scholars believe he was, then he may very well have been familiar with the poem, "A Nosegay Always Sweet, for Lovers to Send for Tokens of Love at New Year's Tide, or for Fairings" thought to have been penned by Hunnis and published in *A Handful of Pleasant Delights* (1584) composed by Clement Robinson "and divers others."

If Violet is for faithfulnesse
Which in me shall abide:
Hoping likewise that from your heart
You will not let it slide.
And will continue in the same
As you have nowe begunne
And then forever to abide
Then you my heart have wonne.

Our seduction by sweet fragrance is nothing new and "violets were always grown in the physic gardens from ancient and medieval times to Colonial and Victorian days."[3] The idea of paradise–of fertile, green, and abundant space; of an Eden where we come to play, to feast, and to nourish ourselves–has existed in the dreams and daily existence of humans from as far back as our memory extends.

Of all the fragrant herbs I send,
none can compare in nobleness with the purple violet.
– 6th century bishop, Fortunatus to his friend,
the abbess queen, Radegonde

We study ancient gardens, plants, and gardeners because the cultivation of plants and the design and maintenance of not only garden plots, vineyards, and orchards but also of pleasure gardens or healing spaces has played an extraordinary role in the body-mind-spiritual state of human beings. In fact, Carroll suggests "the term *kirimabu*, meaning 'pleasure garden', was introduced by Sargon II in the late eighth century BC."[4]

As for the quote about "violets were always grown...." this is a direct quote that comes from: Rosetta E. Clarkson, *Magic Gardens*, page 9.

The Greek botanist, Theophrastus (371–286 B.C.E.), who wrote extensively on plants, lists white violets among his favourite flowers for wreaths and garlands.[5] Violets peek out in the foreground below other flowering plants such as roses, poppies, and Madonna lilies in a garden painting from the Casa del Bracciale d'Oro in Pompeii [see illustration, p. 92]. About twenty years before his death in 1260, the Dominican theologian and scientist Albertus Magnus, also known as Saint Albert the Great, set guidelines for making a pleasure garden. It specifies the planting of "every sweet-smelling herb such as rue, and sage and basil, and likewise all sorts of flowers, as the violet, columbine, lily, rose, iris and the like."[6]

From a 14th century medical poem, twenty-four herbs for healing are

Illustration #1 Fresco.
Casa del Bracciale d'Oro, Pompeii. *Public Domain, Wikipedia*

Illustration #2 Unicorn.
The Hunt of the Unicorn, The Cloisters, New York; from the late 1400s, Paris. *Public Domain, Wikipedia*

described including betony, marigold, pimpernel, periwinkle, rose, lily, sage, rue, fennel, and violet. The end of Medieval times saw a growing interest in flowers and the idea of planting for "pleasance" or pleasure and The Hunt of the Unicorn tapestries vividly underscore that transition away from the concept that gardens were only for practical use. These exquisite works of art overflow with plants that were alive and thriving during the Medieval Ages, and violets are front and center in the enclosure with the unicorn. The tapestries, now hanging in The Cloisters, New York, were designed in Paris at the end of the fifteenth century and are woven in wool, gold, and silk [see illustration #2 Unicorn. Notice the violets above the unicorn's rump.].

By the mid- to late-16th century and into the 17th century, complicated knot designs were being transferred from embroidery to gardens. Here, again, violets take their place along with acanthus, amaranth, asphodels, cornflowers, cowslips and daffodils, daisies, hollyhocks, iris, lilies, marigolds, mint, pansies, peonies, periwinkle, poppies, primroses, snapdragons, stocks, sweet marjoram, sweet William, and wallflowers. Yet again, three kinds of violets are among the flowers included in one of the first shipments of the Massachusetts Company to New England. From the book, *Gardens of Colony and State*, we learn that anemones, carnations and clove pinks, columbine, crown imperial, daffodils, stocks, grape hyacinths, hollyhocks, houseleeks, marigolds, Martagon lilies, honesty, primroses, single and double roses, scarlet cross, sedums, Star of Bethlehem, tulips, violets and yellow daylilies were growing in gardens of the New World prior to 1700.[7]

John Evelyn, the seventeenth century diarist, recommended for "spring fever" a favourite violet dish, which might be a shadowy ancestor of the modern candied violets. He says in his *Acetaria* (1699) that "tansy, qualified with violets, at the entrance of spring fried brownish and eaten with Orange or Lemon Juice and Sugar is one of the most agreeable of all the herbaceous dishes."[8]

Nowadays, we may not have access to the kind of harvest an Elizabethan housewife might require–4 pounds of orange flowers for orange flower water; a bushel of roses for potpourri; 1000 damask roses for "sweet water of the best kind," a pound of rosebuds for oil of roses, a pound of violet flowers for sirup of violets[9]–but a woodland stroll in spring should yield enough violet flowers to enjoy in many ways, including the soothing violet balm in the following recipe.

Violet Balm

Both the Roman Goddess Venus and Empress Josephine Bonaparte (1763 –1814) were partial to the fragrance of sweet violets. Bring out your inner royal with this liltingly light sweet violet oil. Use it as a daily moisturizer or to soothe inflamed skin, rashes, hives, and eczema.

Makes about 1 cup

2 cups violet leaves
1 cup violet flowers
1 cup coconut oil

Line 2 rimmed baking sheets with clean tea towels or paper towels. Spread leaves and flowers in one layer over the sheets and cover with paper towels. Set aside in a warm, dark place to reduce the moisture. The leaf and flower material doesn't have to be crisp-dry.

Combine coconut oil and the slightly dried violet leaves and flowers in a small slow cooker. Turn heat to low, cover and set aside for 6 to 8 hours.

Unplug the cooker, leave the lid on and allow the mixture to cool enough to handle. Pour into smaller, wide-mouth jars, label, and store in a cool cupboard for up to 1 year.

Footnotes
[1] Sinclair Rohde, *The Scented Garden*, page 31.
[2] Bremness, *Essential Herbs*, page 152.
[3] Clarkson, *Magic Gardens*, page 9.
[4] Carroll, *Earthly Paradises*, page 19.
[5] Carroll, ibid, page 88.
[6] Bayard, *Sweet Herbs and Sundry Flowers*, page 11.
[7] Wright, *The Story of Gardening*, page 262 cites *Gardens of Colony and State*, edited by Mrs. L. V.
[8]. Clarkson, *Magic Gardens*, page 9.
[9] Clarkson, ibid, page 151.

Pensée Les fleurs animées, J.J. Grandville, M. Maubert, Illustrator.
Project Gutenberg License, www.gutenberg.org

References

Bayard, Tania. *Sweet Herbs and Sundry Flowers: Medieval Gardens and the Gardens of The Cloisters*. David R. Godine, 1985.

Bayard, Tania, translator and editor. *A Medieval Home Companion: Housekeeping in the Fourteenth Century*. HarperCollins, 1991.

Bremness, Lesley. *Essential Herbs*. Quadrile, 2000. Article heading quote, page 6.

Carroll, Maureen. *Earthly Paradises: Ancient Gardens in History and Archaeology*. The British Museum Press, 2003.

Clarkson, Rosetta E. *Magic Gardens: A Modern Chronicle of Herbs and Savory Seeds*. MacMillan, 1939.

Gordon, Lesley. *Green Magic: Flowers, Plants, and Herbs in Lore and Legend*. Viking Press, 1977.

Hieatt, Constance B. and Sharon Butler. *Pleyn Delit: Medieval Cookery for Modern Cooks*. University of Toronto Press, 1976.

Landsberg, Sylvia. *The Medieval Garden*. The British Museum Press, 1996.

Sinclair Rohde, Eleanour. *The Scented Garden*. The Medici Society, 1931.

Wright, Richardson. *The Story of Gardening*. Dover Publications, 1963. (Unabridged copy of Wright's 1934 work, first published by Dodd, Mead and Company).

No shrinking violet, **Pat Crocker's** mission in life is to channel sweet, white violet energy. Author of 24 cookbooks, Crocker holds a degree in Food, Nutrition, Consumer, and Family Studies (Ryerson University, Toronto) and is a culinary herbalist with more than 1.25 million books in print and several translated into over 11 languages. She was honored twice by the International Herb Association and received the 2009 Gertrude H. Foster award from the Herb Society of America for Excellence in Herbal Literature. Her books, *The Juicing Bible* and *The Vegan Cook's Bible* (both published by Robert Rose) have won "Best in the World" awards from the International Gourmand Culinary Guild.

Read about violets as a flavoring for liqueurs in Pat's book, *The Herbalist's Kitchen* (Sterling Epicure), now available in bookstores everywhere and on her website, www.patcrocker.com

Blooms found at Dow Gardens in Midland, Michigan. *Heather Cohen*

Wild Pansy and Wood Violet, Charles Rennie Mackintosh, 1910.
Public Domain

The Art and Language of *Viola*

Skye Suter

Violets and pansies are part of the larger bouquet of flowers and herbs that speak to us through the language of flowers. They speak to us through mythology and folklore as well as the food and medicine we make from them. The color violet, in all the shades and hues of purple, gives us different messages through variety and application. A Purple Heart is a medal, a physical symbol of bravery, while a purple bruise is something that hurts for a while and says you've got a bad bump, but it will disappear soon. Humans love to name children after flowers; both Violet and Pansy are popular names for girls. Whether it is a painting of flowers in a vase or a vase of flowers on a table, violets and pansies and all other flowers are speaking to us through their own language.

Once you start looking for them, violets and pansies appear everywhere. I have found them dressing up ladies' hats, illuminating the pages of ancient manuscripts, ornamenting vases, dangling from earrings and necklaces, and depicted in fine art paintings. There is even a restaurant in my town named Violette's Cellar with the exterior painted in violets.

During Victorian times small bouquets of pleasant-smelling herbs and flowers, enfolded in a doily, were called tussie-mussies. During this period young people in love were particularly fond of using flowers to send messages to each other. A fellow might give his beloved a bouquet with a honey flower (a flower with abundant nectar) and a pansy to mean "I am thinking of our forbidden love," or "I am feeling amorous towards you," or "I have been missing you." In these times the pansy was often employed in presentations of secretive courting or displays of love. Overt displays of passion were severely frowned upon, so romantic communications were confined to convoluted messages done in flowers, which were then deciphered using small dictionaries or code books.

The name *pansy* comes from the French word *pensée* for thought, and since ancient times it has been a symbol of remembrance. The pansy is often used

Thoughtful Pansy. Skye Suter

as a get-well flower to show sympathy and empathy toward the pain and distress of another. Pansies symbolize loving feelings, yet also represent free thinking and deliberation. The word "pensée" is the past tense of "to think" but is also a feminine reflexive, which led to the word *pansy* being used as a pejorative insinuation to describe a man who is too womanly.

When we look to the age of myths, we find the violet speaking to us in the language of flowers through handed down tales. Why does a flower grow in a certain place, in a certain manner, or at a particular time of year? Myths and folk stories have always explained natural phenomena and occurrences in ways that were logical to people from long ago. In modern times we will give our mother or loved one a bouquet of violets, without comprehending or even thinking about the historic reasons for the gesture.

In the Greek language, the word for *violet* is *Ion. Ione* also means a violet-colored stone. The daughter of the king of Argos, named *Io,* had the misfortune to catch the eye of Zeus (or the Roman Jupiter) who pursued her as his next love conquest. To hide Io from his jealous wife Hera, Zeus turned Io into a white cow and created sweet violets for her to eat. The violet grows low to the ground, with sweet purple or white flowers, nice for grazing cows. The Greeks believed violets were sacred to Io and to the god Ares.

A similar tale is the Iroquois legend of chase, conquest, love, and death. A famous warrior fell in love with a maiden from an enemy tribe and carried her off. The opposing tribe caught up with them and slayed the lovers where they lay–causing the first blue violets to spring up, thus making the violet a symbol of constant love, for youthful warriors and maidens to pick and smell in the springtime. Because of the love connection in various myths and stories (and the fact that it flowers in the earlier part of spring), the violet has become a symbol of spring.

There are other ancient explanations for the presence of the violet, such as the flower springing up where Orpheus laid his enchanted lute, or Venus (the goddess of love) thrashing a group of girls and turning them into violets simply because her son Cupid declared them more beautiful than Venus. The very existence, habit, and color of the violet have been explained by these and other similar narratives.

American pioneers thought that a handful of violets taken into the farmhouse in spring insured a prosperous household. Neglecting this ritual would bring harm to the baby chicks and ducklings of spring. I can't see why one would avoid bringing these lovely flowers into the home–they are attractive, sweet smelling, and speak to us of spring.

In England it was believed that periwinkle (*Vinca minor)* eaten by husband and wife would cause them to love one another. Though not true violets, periwinkle has violet-colored blooms and was sometimes called "Sorcerer's Violet" for its frequent use in the manufacture of charms against the Evil Eye and malevolent spirits. The French knew it as the *Violette des Sorciers*, and the Italians as *Centocchio*, or Hundred Eyes.

We get to understand plants and appreciate their gifts to us by using our senses: touch, smell, taste, vision, and even hearing. The creation of a garland of fresh flowers, the making of a tea, or the painting of a picture requires us to make use of all our senses.

Imagine a day spent sensing the violet:

Seeing Violet
The violet bids you to admire its pretty blooms in shades of purple, yellow and white. Coming upon a group of violets, you might pick a few for a vase. Perhaps you might be moved to press a few of these flowers in the pages of a book, or take pen to paper and create an image or prose inspired by the violet.

Hearing Violet
You might hear violet in the picking of the plant or the sipping of the tea you just made with steeped violet blossoms. Chewing the blossom can create a squeak of your teeth or a crunch if it is candied. You might hear violet calling to you in the breeze, to smell and look at it.

Smelling Violet
You might then smell that violet and be motivated to pick a bouquet of scented violets. The wild violet has a fragrance that has encouraged perfumers to gather them for the same reason.

Touching Violet
Violet petals are soft. Seeing them inspires touching them because they look so soft and velvety–but gently, so they won't wither, as they are as delicate as a butterfly wing. The violet tells you to pick a handful with a few little heart-shaped leaves and put them in a little vase, to visualize the softness of the blossoms for a longer length of time. When one eats the blossoms decorating a cake this softness of the blossoms can be felt.

Tasting Violet

At the end of the day, you might want to take a few of those violets that have been sitting prettily in a vase and make them into a tea. Though leaves and flowers are used for tea, the leaves are stronger flavored. To make tea from the fresh flowers, use around two tablespoons of blossoms for one cup.

According to some experts, yellow violets can cause gastric distress, so use the other colors.

Plants in religion were used to symbolize sacred ideas. Plants that represent the Trinity have the number three in common, for the Father, the Son, and the Holy Spirit. The "three" can be leaves of three or triangular shapes. The pansy also represents pious humility. From the poet and author, Bret Harte we have: "From brute beasts' humility I learned;/ And the pansy's life God's providence discerned." Herb Trinity, or the wild pansy, *V. tricolor*, is one of the plants used on Trinity Sunday, and represents the idea of three with its three colors–purple, white, and yellow. These same three colors of heartsease (also a common name for *V. tricolor*), symbolize memories and loving thoughts.

In Christian symbolism the violet has always stood for the valued virtues of humbleness, humility, and modesty, and was thus associated with virgins and saints. It is said that violets grew on the graves of these revered persons and that is why violets are associated with death and mourning. Violets are also associated with the Virgin Mother Mary, and white violets symbolize purity and faithfulness.

A mother's devotion to her family is often honored with a bouquet of flowers on Mother's Day and can include the modest and sweet-smelling violet. Queen Victoria was quite dedicated to this deferential little flower and mentioned it many times in her copious diary entries. Picture Eliza Doolittle in *My Fair Lady* and *Pygmalion*—she represents the many flower sellers of the time selling small bouquets of fragrant sweet violets to passing ladies and gentlemen.

While violets and pansies are associated with religion, mothers, and Victorian posey bouquets, they are also found strewn about in literary works and in the visual arts. In the works of Shakespeare there are numerous references to the *Viola* family.

Some plants which are not violas take on color names in the purple family, such as periwinkle and lavender. The color violet is derived from the flower of the same name and is often used interchangeably with the word *purple*. The colors purple or violet stand for ambition, luxury, royalty, power, nobility, grandeur, creativity, and wisdom.

Flower names are often used to name our children, both girls and boys. The daughter of the 60s singer Donovan is named Ione Skye; "Ione" is an alternative to "Violet." Violet and Pansy are both used to name girls. In the language of flowers, "violet" implies modesty and compliance, but today the name Violet is simply for the flower or the color. The girl's name "Pansy" describes a girl who is more fun-loving and tomboyish. So, if a girl is named Violet or Pansy, does she become demure or tomboyish on her own, or is the influence coming from the desires of the parents? The idea of matching humans and flowers with certain characteristics are prepackaged ideas, sent to us through beliefs and interpretations from ages ago.

Girls' flower names are found in classic shows and books. In the television show *Keeping Up Appearances*, the female sisters of the family all have flower names and characteristics that reflect those names. Hyacinth Bucket, the main character, is bossy, over-scented, and out there. Her sister Daisy sort of flops all over the place and is a bit on the sloppy side, while sister Rose is putting herself out for a show. And lastly, sister Violet lives up to her name by never being seen.

Artistic expression with violets and pansies takes many forms. A sweet syrup for pancakes, a perfume, a tea, a pressed flower, or a flower arrangement are all ways of immortalizing and remembering your favorite flowers. In the visual arts, representations of violets and pansies run the gamut from Victorian era postcards to fine art paintings by famous artists.

Portrait of Berthe Morisot with a Bouquet of Violets (1872) is a famous Impressionist painting by artist Édouard Manet of one of his favorite models. In the painting, Morisot, also an Impressionist painter, is dressed in all black and is holding a barely perceptible bouquet of violets.

In the famous painting of Ophelia (1851-52) by Sir John Everett Millais, you can clearly see a purple violet and a wild pansy in the scattering of flowers drifting in the river with the slowly drowning Ophelia. If you happen to go to London, you can view this painting at the Tate Gallery; otherwise, you can find it online. A good rendition: https://en.wikipedia.org/ wiki/Ophelia_(painting)#/media/File:John_Everett_Millais_-_Ophelia_-_ Google_Art_Project.jpg.

Ophelia (1851-52). Sir John Everett Millais, Tate Britain, London. *Wikipedia*

Pansies Playtime. Victorian Ad Trade Card, The Standard Sewing Machine Company. *Public Domain*

P is for Pansy. Vintage Print, Cicely Mary Barker, 1930. *Public Domain*

The Scottish designer and artist Charles Rennie Mackintosh was renowned for his work in the Art Nouveau and Arts and Crafts movements. He produced numerous flower studies including *Wild Pansy and Wood Violet* (1910), rendered in pencil and watercolor.

Violets and pansies frequently decorated postcards from the mid-nineteenth century into the twentieth century. Although many cards were decorated with beautiful and realistic flowers, some depicted quirky personifications of flowers and animals. While violets seem to have been in the minority when it came to Victorian postcard personifications, pansies were well represented. Probably because it is easy to see an animal or human face in the wide-open face of the pansy flower.

Fantasy illustration comes into play with interpretations of imaginary beings like fairies and pixies. Fairies and flowers have had a mutually long and happy association. Victorians were enchanted with the ideas of fairies and associated them with flowers, plants, and woodland settings. Fairies have often been depicted alongside flowers or represented as anthropomorphic flowers. A fine example is the letter *P is for Pansy* from of a set of antique alphabet cards, which illustrate letters of the alphabet with fairies dressed in flowers, whose names start with each letter. Personified postcard pansies are plentiful—and adorable! Many endearing images with little lion-like pansy faces and human forms can be found on postcards from this era.

People have always seen human forms and characteristics in the organic forms of flowers and plants. Books and artworks from the Golden Age of Illustration (1800s) show numerous examples of animated flowers and flower gardens. *Flowers from Shakespeare's Garden,* designed and illustrated by the great Walter Crane, is an album filled with fanciful personifications of flowers and herbs based on the bard's works. Both violet and pansy are represented in this album. Crane illustrates the violet with Shakespeare's line: "Violets, dim, / But sweeter than the lids of Juno's eyes...." The pansy illustration is accompanied with "... and there is pansies, that's for thoughts," part of Shakespeare's famous "rosemary for remembrance" stanza.

To me, the illustrations of J.J. Grandville epitomize the personification of flowers in human form. The book, *Les Fleurs Animées* or *The Court of Flora*, was published posthumously in the year of his death, in 1847. Grandville was a French caricaturist and artist who made his name through the publication of illustrated lithographic albums.

In the book, each of Grandville's fifty-two illustrations are accompanied by dialogue on the facing page. The plates include flowers from cultivated gardens as well as in the fields. He does not claim any scientific accuracy but considers his illustrations to be fanciful interpretations. Attributes, symbolism, and storylines are described through words and illustrations for each of the flowers, much in the way we have come to understand them through historical reference.

For example, the *Pansy* is leaning against an urn, deep in pensive thought, dressed in a gown of pansies. The accompanying story describes poor Pansy as searching for lodgings and being continually turned away until she finds shelter with an admiring poet who sees her as a positive presence. (See page 95 for this thoughtful pansy illustration.)

The illustration *Violet* shows a group of violets modestly grouped together, sitting demurely in the shade of violet leaves. They are holding incense burners that give off their own scent of violets. They are further described by the character, Count Felix, "This charming flower, need we say, is the emblem of modest merit...."

I have long taken inspiration from Grandville's *Court of Flora* and other similar illustrations to create my own drawings of herbal pixies and fairies over the years, and plan to continue to do so in the future.

Sweet Violets. *www.freevintageart.com*

References

Beasley, Toby. "In Search of Queen Victoria's Favorite Flower." *English Heritage.* https://blog.english-heritage.org.uk/in-search-of-queen-victorias-favourite-flower/. Accessed June 13, 2021.

Crane, Walter. *Flowers from Shakespeare's Garden: a Posy from the Plays, pictured by Walter Crane.* Macmillan Publishing Co. Inc., 1980.

Folkard, Richard. *Plant Lore Legends and Lyrics; Embracing the Myths, Traditions, Superstitions, and Folk-Lore of the Plant Kingdom.* Project Gutenberg eBook. Release date: January 2014. eBook #44638.

Grandville, J.J. *The Court of Flora, Les Fleurs Animées-The Engraved Illustrations of J.J. Grandville.* George Braziller, Inc., 1981.

"And there is Pansies, that's for Thoughts." *Pansies for Plato.* https://pansiesforplato.wordpress.com/and-there-is-pansies-thats-for-thoughts/. Accessed May 24, 2021.

"Ophelia's Flowers" *A Shakespeare Garden; Inspiration to help you create your own Shakespeare garden, discussing both plant-lore and flower symbolism.* https://bardgarden.blogspot.com/2015/01/ophelias-flowers.html. Accessed May 24, 2021.

Posted by tequalelu in *Myth.* "Legend of the Violet." *Herbe Rowe.* https://herberowe.wordpress.com/2011/02/14/legend-of-the-violet/. Accessed June 13, 2021.

Skye Suter broadcasts her fondness for art and plants through several disciplines. As a writer and illustrator, she contributes to the International Herb Association's annual Herb of the Year ™ publication and other free-lance projects. Skye pens plant-themed articles, lectures on herbs and related subjects to interested groups, and produces a series of newsletters and bulletins, including a monthly newsletter for the Staten Island Herb Society, a quarterly newsletter for the International Herb Association, and a seasonal bulletin for Friends of Blue Heron Park, Inc.

Visit Skye's website anherballeaf.com to view her publications, *An Herbal Leaf Journal,* and *An Herbal Leaf Monthly Message*–newsletters which reflect an interest in "plants, nature, art, crafting, cooking, and especially herbs." An archived section to *An Herbal Leaf* website contains past issues of Monthly Messages and Journals, and is available on the website through a subscription. Skye can be reached at anherballeaf@gmail.com.

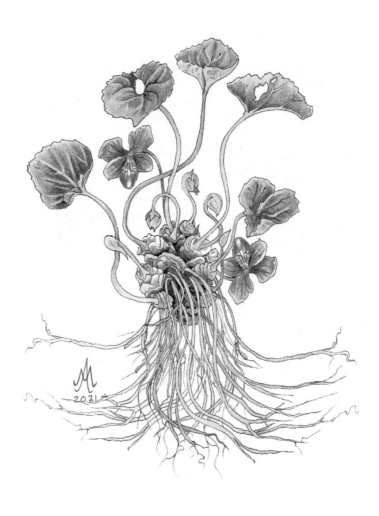

Alicia Mann

Violets in the Kitchen

Just-candied violets set to dry and harden. *Susan Belsinger*

Crystallized Edible Flowers & Herb Leaves

Susan Belsinger

Candied flowers have been used for centuries as confections and garnishes for all sort of desserts from wedding cakes and cupcakes to custards and petit fours. Violets and rose petals are the most popular candied flowers. I have had them in France, where they can be found already candied and packed in beribboned jars. One brand uses colored pink and violet-hued sugars to accentuate the colors of the rose petals and violas.

Besides the violas—violets, Johnny jump-ups, and pansy petals—good candidates for candying are apple or plum blossoms, borage flowers, lilac florets, rose petals, and scented geraniums. Rose petals should be separated. When candying leaves, use small, thin ones—I like lemon balm, mint, and anise hyssop leaves. This job takes a little patience; it seems to go more quickly if you do it with a friend (and a lovely libation). The following recipe will coat quite a few flowers—if you need more, mix up a second batch. If you are concerned about using a raw egg white, powdered pasteurized egg whites are available in the grocery and they work just fine.

There are two ways to handle the little flowers: leave them on the stem or remove the stem. If you leave them on the stem, then you can hold them by the stem and when you finish egg-washing and sugaring, you can place them on the parchment paper face-side down and snip the stem off. If you remove the stem beforehand, then you will need to hold the flowers with tweezers when handling them.

Rinsed and dried flower blossoms and/or herb leaves
1 extra-large egg white, at room temperature
Few drops of water
About 1 cup superfine sugar

You will need to have a small paint brush or two, wax or parchment paper, and a baking rack. Spread the wax or parchment paper on the baking rack.

In a small bowl combine the egg white with the water and beat lightly with a fork or small whisk until the white just shows a few bubbles. Put the sugar in a shallow dish.

Holding a leaf, flower, or petal in one hand (by stem or with tweezers), dip a paint brush into the egg white and gently paint it. Cover the leaf or flower completely, though not excessively; it should be wet all over, but not dripping.

Hold the leaf or flower over the sugar dish and gently sprinkle sugar evenly all over on both sides. Place the leaf or flower on the wax or parchment paper to dry. Continue with the rest of the leaves and flowers.

Let the leaves and flowers dry completely, they should be free of moisture. This could take 12 to 36 hours depending on atmospheric humidity. Generally, I put the tray on top of the refrigerator overnight and then check them. If they are sufficiently dried on the one side, I gently turn them (use a thin tool or knife if need be) and let the downward-facing side dry. To hasten drying, the candied flowers can be placed in an oven overnight with a pilot light, or oven light turned on.

Store the dried, candied flowers in airtight containers between layers of wax paper or parchment until ready to use. They can be kept for up to 1 year.

Pat Kenny

Everything you need to crystalize edible flowers: egg whites, sugar, small paintbrushes and edible blooms. *Susan Belsinger*

Close-up of candied pansy. *Susan Belsinger*

Gourmet breakfast: easy-to-make omelet with chives, violet leaves and flowers. *Susan Belsinger*

Omelet with Violet Leaves & Flowers

Violets work delightfully well in this omelet—it is tasty as well as quite attractive. I added fresh chives; use either common or garlic chives. The recipe is adapted from the Violet Omelet from the article "Violets in the Kitchen" by Peter Gail published in the Fall 1996/Winter 1997 issue of <u>Sweet Times: A Journal for the Genus Viola by the International Violet Association</u>. Have your garnishes set aside, your bread toasting, your tea or coffee steeping, and your plate warming while preparing the omelet.

Serves 1

9 or 10 violet leaves
9 or 10 violet flowers
Fresh snipped chives, 5 or 6 leaves
2 extra-large eggs
1 tablespoon half-and-half cream, milk or cream
About 2 teaspoons butter
About 1 generous tablespoon freshly grated Parmesan cheese
Salt and freshly ground black pepper

Rinse the violet leaves, flowers and chives if need be and pat dry. Chiffonade the violet leaves, saving a few whole for garnish. Remove the violets from their stems. Snip the chives into a little bowl.

In a small bowl, beat the eggs with a fork, add the half-and-half and combine well.

Melt the butter in a small omelet pan over medium-low heat. Pour the egg and cream mixture into the hot pan. Run a spatula around and under the edge of the omelet to loosen. Sprinkle the Parmesan over the omelet and cover for a minute or two. Remove the lid and scatter the prepared leaves, half of the flowers and most of the chives (leave a few for garnish) over the omelet. Season lightly with salt and pepper.

When the egg is just set on top, fold the omelet in from both sides to form a roll. Serve the omelet on a warmed plate with toast, scone or biscuit. Garnish the omelet with the remaining violets and a scattering of snipped chives, and the plate with a few violet leaves. Serve immediately.

References

Belsinger, Susan. 1991. *Flowers in the Kitchen: A Bouquet of Tasty Recipes*. Loveland, Colorado: Interweave Press.

Belsinger, Susan. 2005. *not just desserts—sweet herbal recipes*. Brookeville, Maryland: herbspirit.

Susan Belsinger bio on page 6

Vibrant blue-violet blooms. *Susan Belsinger*

Versatile Violets

Pat Crocker

Versatile violets can be added to many dishes. A woodland stroll in spring should yield enough violet flowers to enjoy in the following recipes.

Violet Cordial

Traditionally, a cordial was taken to strengthen the heart and so my spring cordial recipe below pairs young hawthorn buds and flowers with vibrantly purple violets.

Makes about a pint

1/3 cup unsweetened pomegranate juice
1/2 cup honey
2 cups violet flowers
2 cups hawthorn buds and/or flowers
2 tablespoons fresh or dried hibiscus flowers
1 apple, skin on, seeds removed
1 teaspoon minced fresh ginger
3 cardamom pods, crushed
1 vanilla bean, cut in half lengthwise
1 2-inch cinnamon stick
Zest of 1 lemon
2 cups brandy

Combine pomegranate juice and honey in a saucepan and bring to a boil, stirring frequently over medium-high heat.

Meanwhile, toss violet, hawthorn, and hibiscus flowers together in a bowl. Pour boiling juice over, stir well and set aside to cool.

Chop apple into a quart jar. Add ginger, cardamom, vanilla, cinnamon, lemon zest, and brandy. Place the lid on the jar and shake well. While the syrup is still warm, add it to the jar, scraping the wilted flowers and all dregs into the jar. Replace the lid and shake to mix the ingredients.

Label and set the jar in a cool, dark place for 4 weeks and shake it every couple of days. Strain the liquid into a smaller jar and discard the solids.

Label and store the cordial in a dark, cool cupboard for up to 6 months or for 1 year in the refrigerator.

Violet Broth

Violets were a regular item on the Mediaeval menu—they were chopped up with onions and lettuce for a salad or cooked with fennel and savory for broth. This is my interpretation of a rich spring broth to cleanse our systems of winter's heavier fare. You can sip the broth alone or tramp around in woods and fields for some wild-foraged ingredients such as violets, nettles, wild leeks, wild ginger, and perhaps some marsh marigold.

Serves 4 to 6

For the broth
Avocado or olive oil in a spritzer bottle
1 large yellow onion, skin on, quartered
1 slice, 1-inch-thick green cabbage
4 cloves garlic, skin on, smashed
6 brown crimini mushrooms, quartered
1 apple, skin on, quartered, seeds removed
8 cups water
2 tablespoons tamari sauce
2 tablespoons miso
2 tablespoons nutritional yeast
2 tablespoons chive or herb vinegar

For the soup
10 fresh wild leeks, white and green, chopped
1 cup chopped fennel bulb
1 cup fresh nettle leaves
1/2 cup fresh violet flowers or flowers and leaves
1/4 cup chopped fresh savory
1 tablespoon chopped fresh wild ginger
1/2 cup fresh young wild marsh marigold flowers and leaves, optional
Ramen noodles (2 servings size package)

To make the broth: Spritz or lightly oil the bottom of a large stockpot with oil. Heat the pot over high heat for 3 minutes. Stir in the onion and cook, stirring frequently for 5 minutes. Add the cabbage, garlic, mushrooms, and apple and cook, stirring frequently for 7 to 10 minutes or until the vegetables are slightly charred around the edges and the bottom of the pot is slightly browned.

Add the water and bring it to a boil. Reduce heat and simmer the broth for 3 to 5 hours, adding another cup of water if the liquid is reduced by more than half.

Turn the heat off and let the broth cool in the pot on the stove. Strain broth into a large bowl through a fine metal strainer. Discard the solids and return the broth to the pot. Bring to a light simmer over medium-high heat and add the tamari sauce, miso, nutritional yeast and vinegar. Taste and add more tamari if required.

To make the soup: Add the leeks, fennel, nettle leaves, violets, savory, ginger, and marsh marigold, if using, to the simmering broth. Stir in the noodles and cook, stirring occasionally for 6 minutes or until the noodles are cooked, the onions are tender, and the greens are wilted.

Violet Pudding

15th century cooks made violet fritters and a kind of custard called "mon ami," which was garnished with violets. This recipe is adapted from the recipe for Red Rose Pudding, Pleyn Delit.

Serves 4 to 6

1 cup dried or candied violet flowers
2 tablespoons rice flour or cornstarch
2 cups almond milk, divided
1/4 cup sugar
1/4 teaspoon salt
1/4 cup ground almonds

Pulverize violets to a powder using a mortar and pestle or small spice grinder.

Combine rice flour with 3 tablespoons of the milk in a small bowl and transfer to a blender. Add violet powder, sugar, and salt. Blend until smooth. With the motor running, slowly add the remaining milk and the almonds and blend until smooth.

Transfer to a heavy saucepan and heat over medium-high heat, stirring constantly for about 5 minutes or until the pudding is thickened.

Pour into a serving bowl or 4 to 6 individual dessert bowls. Cover with plastic wrap and chill.

References

Hieatt, Constance B. and Sharon Butler. *Pleyn Delit: Medieval Cookery for Modern Cooks*. University of Toronto Press, 1976.

Pat Crocker bio page 96

Crème de Violette ~ Violet Liqueur

Karen England

Who bends a knee where violets grow,
a hundred secret things shall know.
- Rachel Field

There is a classic liqueur made from fragrant violet petals called *Crème de Violette* that is probably one of the "hundred secret things" that Rachel Field refers to. It is the basis for many a popular violet-flavored cocktail found on the menus of trendy bars and restaurants. Not only can you make these violet-flavored cocktails at home, but you can also make the liqueur yourself. Another classic liqueur, also made with violets, is *Crème de Yvette* but it contains berries and other ingredients and is not made solely of violets. Using *Crème de Yvette* instead of *Crème de Violette* in cocktail recipes calling for *Violette* is a common practice but not recommended, as the flavors are very different.

If you are growing violets, be advised that the more fragrant the variety, such as *Viola odorata,* and the darker the flower color, the better the liqueur you will make and ultimately the cocktails you make with it.

I grow Australian violets, *Viola hederacea,* which are pale in color and faint of scent, and the flavor they give to a liqueur is very vegetal even with all the stems and green calyxes removed. If you are growing fragrant violets, before making the DIY recipe, increase your floral flavor by removing each green calyx and stem, which will otherwise add an unwanted grassy flavor to the finished product.

If the violets you are growing are not fragrant, do as I do and purchase food-grade, dried violets (I bought mine online) and use those for making liqueur.

When purchasing commercial violet liqueurs or ordering violet cocktails when out on the town, remember that "violet-flavored" is different than "violet-colored." There are many violet-named drinks named solely for the

Blue Moon Cocktail, glass rimmed with crushed crystallized violets.
Karen England

color that have no violet flowers in them, and even some that are not violet-colored either, as is the case with the "Lady Violet" drink, most likely named for a woman named Violet, which is a clear, colorless beverage sans any violet flavor.

Homemade Crème de Violette

Vodka is preferred for this liqueur because it is flavorless, but historically brandy was used to make some brands of commercial Crème de Violette. Parma Violette Candies, which are similar to American SweeTarts but with a violet flavor, popular in the UK, are often dissolved in gin to make something called Parma Violet Gin. The following recipe can be easily doubled or tripled if you have enough violet flowers. If you add a mixture of berries— blackberries, raspberries, strawberries—plus some vanilla bean and orange peel to the alcohol portion of the recipe along with the violets, and then add some honey to the syrup portion, you will have a homemade version of Crème de Yvette.

1/2 cup fresh or dried fragrant violet flowers, stems and green calyxes removed. The more flowers the better!
1/2 cup or more vodka, brandy or gin, enough to cover 1/4 cup (half) of the violet flowers
1/4 to 1/2 cup granulated sugar, enough to layer with the other 1/4 cup of the flowers
1/8 to 1/4 cup distilled water
Optional: lemon juice, approximately 1 to 2 teaspoons

Sterilize two pint-size mason jars.

Divide the flowers in half. Layer the first half of the flowers in one mason jar with sugar until all the flowers are covered. In the other mason jar cover the other half of the flowers with vodka. Note: If you are a baker or candy maker, save some of this after straining, but before sweetening, to use as violet extract in cookie, cake, and candy recipes.

Seal both the jars and set aside for a few days. After a few days, put the sugar and violets from the first jar into a saucepan and add approximately 1/8 to 1/4 cup distilled water (about half the amount of water as the amount of sugar used.) Heat all just to dissolve the sugar and make it syrupy, but don't boil. Cool. Set aside. (Before proceeding with making the liqueur, refrigerate a portion of this violet simple syrup separately to use in cocktails later.)

Use a strainer to remove the flowers from the syrup and alcohol. In a quart mason jar (or new or reused glass bottle), cleaned and sterilized, combine the syrup and alcohol. Shake well to mix thoroughly. If you wish to add lemon juice, be prepared—the color (and flavor) will change slightly. Seal and set aside for a week before using.

Aviation

I couldn't resist getting a new-to-me gin for this recipe called, wait for it... "McQueen and the Violet Fog"—I kid you not, that's the name! It's delicious, and there is also a gin called Aviation, named for this drink ... but just pick a gin you like.

Yield: one drink

2 ounces gin
1/2 ounce Maraschino Liqueur or cherried brandy liquid (see following recipe)
1/4 ounce *Crème de Violette* (use a splash more if using homemade)
1/2 to 3/4 ounce fresh lemon juice, depending on how sweet you want the drink
Brandied cherry, for garnish (see following recipe)
Fresh pansy, viola, or Johnny-jump-up blossoms for garnish

Stir everything but the cherry together with lots of ice until well chilled. Strain into a chilled coupe glass and garnish with a cherry (or two; I saw an interview with a hundred-year-old woman who, when asked the secret to her long life, said "I always have several cherries in my cocktails because you never know how long you'll live.") and some fresh pansies, violas, or Johnny-jump-up flowers.

Brandied Cherries

If you make the following recipe for homemade brandied cherries to use for the garnish, then also use their cherried brandy liquid instead of the Maraschino liqueur in the Aviation cocktail.

I rely on a recipe by Amanda Schuster from alcoholprofessor.com that I augment with a vanilla bean and bay leaves. I can't grow cherries in my climate, so I look at the farmers market for cherries in season with long stems; because I leave the stems on, they act as handles and look fetching in a drink. I leave the stones in—I do not pit my cocktail cherries. The pits add a nutty essence that is outstanding, something that you do not get, even with the addition of almond extract, when using pitted cherries. However, if the stems and pits bother you, then remove them.

Each variety of cherry will make a different end product, but they are all good, so use what you grow or can get.

1/2 cup sugar, preferably organic
1/2 cup distilled water
1 stick cinnamon
Grated fresh nutmeg
1 or 2 fresh or dried bay leaves
1 vanilla bean
1 pound of fresh cherries, any kind.
1 cup of good quality brandy
1 teaspoon vanilla extract

To make the syrup: Heat the sugar, water, cinnamon, nutmeg, bay leaves and vanilla bean on low heat for several minutes until the sugar is dissolved and becomes a bit syrupy. Remove from heat.

Add the cherries and coat well with the syrup.

Add the brandy and vanilla extract and stir to coat. Let cool.

Carefully transfer the cherries, then the boozy syrup to a glass jar with lid. Turn it over a couple of times for good measure, then store in refrigerator. Let the cherries steep at least overnight before use.

These will last several months to a year. Use the cherry brandy liqueur in drinks, as well as the cherries. These cherries make great gifts.

Lady In Blue

For this recipe I use Empress 1908 Gin which is naturally an indigo blue color from one of the ingredients, Butterfly Pea Flower. The "Lady" in question will be less blue if you use a clear gin.

If you are using homemade Crème de Violette, use more, to let your hard-won violet flavor shine through.

The original recipe for this drink called for a dollop (splash) of Blue Curaçao (a bitter orange liqueur that is not naturally blue—its makers use food coloring) and 3 drops of orange flower water in the glass. It's delicious made that way, but if you don't have these ingredients, instead use any orange flavored liqueur, such as Triple Sec or Cointreau, you can omit the orange flower water, and use an orange peel for garnish. If you have any heartsease flowers handy, float a few on the drink for pizzazz.

Yields one drink

1 1/2 ounce gin
1/4 to 1/2 ounce Crème de Violette
1/2 to 3/4 ounce fresh lemon juice, to taste
1/2 ounce violet honey syrup (see recipe below)
Orange flavored liqueur
Orange flower water (optional)
Orange peel for garnish

To make the violet honey syrup: Combine 1 part water, 2 parts sugar, 1 part fresh or dried violets, and 1 part honey in a saucepan. Heat all together to dissolve the sugar and let steep while cooling. Strain and use... or use the violet simple syrup from the previous Crème de Violette recipe.

Stir together the gin, Crème de Violette, lemon juice, and violet honey syrup with lots of ice until well chilled. Strain into a chilled coupe glass that you have splashed with orange liqueur, the orange flower water, if using; and garnish with a strip of fresh orange peel.

Blue Moon

For this cocktail Empress 1908 Gin is preferred for its natural blue color and deliciousness. For a tarter Blue Moon, use more lemon juice and less liqueur; for a sweeter cocktail, use more liqueur and less lemon.

For the recipe for candied violets, see page 113; "Crystalized Edible Flowers and Herb Leaves" by Susan Belsinger.

Yields one drink

2 ounces gin of choice
1/2 to 3/4 ounce fresh squeezed lemon juice
3/4 to 1 ounce Crème de Violette, to taste
Handful of candied violets (not violet candies), purchased or homemade, crushed to a powder.
1 or 2 brandied cherries (preceding recipe) for garnish, plus pansy, viola, violet and/or Johnny-jump-up blossoms.

Moisten the rim of a chilled coupe glass with lemon juice and dip the rim into the powdered candied violets to coat the edge. Put the sugared glass in the fridge if you are not working quickly to keep it chilled.

Stir the gin, lemon juice and Crème de Violette with lots of ice until well-chilled and strain into the prepared coupe. Garnish with cherries and flowers.

Viola Martinis. *Karen England*

Scotch Violets

Recipe from foodandwine.com by Carey Jones and John D. McCarthy

Yields one drink

2 ounces blended Scotch, such as Cutty Sark Prohibition
1 ounce fresh lemon juice
3/4 to 1 ounce Crème de Violette (Use more liqueur if making this drink with homemade.)
1/4 ounce violet honey syrup (See Lady in Blue recipe.)
Twist of lemon peel, wheel, or wedge for garnish, plus violet flowers

Shake or stir the liquids with lots of ice until very cold. Strain into an old-fashioned glass with fresh ice cubes and garnish.

Karen England grew up working for her cousin's family plant nursery in Encinitas, California, called Sunshine Gardens, but, as a 12-year-old kid in the 1970s she never enjoyed the plants. That is, not until she got married, at the age of 30, and started to learn to cook and garden for herself. While making spaghetti sauce she had an epiphany and, the next day at work, she purchased the herb plants called for in the recipe and went home and planted them. Although she planted them "all wrong," squashed together like canned sardines in the shade, the herbs adjusted to their surroundings and grew! Better than that, they tasted good! That experience over 30 years ago changed Karen's life, sending her on an herbal journey of discovery and made her finally happy to work in such a wonderful family business and industry.

Currently Karen is the president of and managing newsletter editor for the San Diego Horticultural Society and she is owner and operator of Edgehill Herb Farm, a homebased herbal business. She can be found on Instagram @edgehillherbfarm and her blog and store can be found at https://edgehillherbfarm.blog/.

Just-picked tussie mussie of wild violets. *Susan Belsinger*

Smiling *Viola* Faces. *Heather Cohen*

Violas ~ Those Pleasant Faces That Smile Back at You

Donna Frawley

I love violas—violets, pansies, and Johnny-jump-ups. Growing violas is quite easy in Michigan, where I live. Johnny-jump-ups seed themselves in a lot of places, so I have been able to share them with friends. Over the years I have used them more and more in my cooking. I love to think on the meanings of herbs and flowers when I plan a menu, so the foods have additional significance because of which herbs and flowers I use.

According to *Flora's Dictionary–The Victorian Language of Herbs and Flowers*, by Kathleen Gips, the meanings of different violas are:
Johnny-jump-ups: happy thoughts.
Pansy: tender and pleasant thoughts, love, "You occupy my thoughts."
Violet, blue: love, faithfulness, sweetness, loyalty.
Violet, white: modesty, innocence, candor.
Violet, yellow: rural happiness.

Harvesting

To harvest your edible flowers, use a clean, sharp knife or clean scissors. Harvest in the morning before the sun gets too hot but after the dew is gone. Cut the stems long enough so that they have a way to suck up water to keep the flowers fresh. On really hot days bring a container of water out to the garden. Put the flowers in the water as you cut them, so they don't wilt. On cooler days, you can lay flowers in a cake pan or colander, working quickly. Take them immediately inside and use one of the following methods.

Keeping Flowers Fresh

Keeping your flowers fresh after you pick them is important. You don't want to go through all the work of picking them and then have them wilted when it comes time to use them. There are several ways to keep your picked flowers fresh:

Put cut stems in a glass of water either on the counter or in the refrigerator. The flower stems need to be fairly long for them to stay in the water.

Put cut flowers in a zippered bag. Put cut stems in a damp paper towel, fold bottom of towel up so stems are sandwiched between the paper towel, and roll up side-ways, so stems are like a little bouquet. Place carefully in the bag, zip almost all the way closed and blow air in the bag to help cushion the flowers. Then place the bag into the refrigerator.

Flowers with short stems can be put in a foam container (like the ones you get in restaurants for your leftovers) lined with a wet paper towel. Close the lid and store in the refrigerator.

Egg Roll Pasta Using Herbs and Flowers

I have used this recipe many times and really enjoy how the dark colored pansies show through the cooked pasta.

Makes 50 to 100 individual pastas, depending on the size of the flowers.

1 pound wonton or egg roll skins (use what you need and freeze the rest)
3 teaspoons cornstarch
3 tablespoons cold water
Fresh edible flowers (Johnny-jump-ups, nasturtiums, pansies, or sage blossoms)
Fresh herb leaves (sage, salad burnet, Italian parsley, or cilantro)

Combine cornstarch and water in a small bowl, stir with a spoon to dissolve. This will be your "glue." Use a small paint brush to apply a coat of the cornstarch mixture onto one wonton skin. Carefully place a few leaves and/ or flower petals onto the skin. Brush another wonton skin with the cornstarch mixture and place it on top of the first skin. Use a rolling pin to remove air bubbles. Trim the edges with a pastry wheel, a cookie cutter, or a sharp knife. I like to put a pansy flower in the center with a Johnny-jump-up flower in each corner and cut them each out with cookie cutters that are a little larger than the flower. They can be 1 to 2 1/2 inches.

Set finished pasta squares onto a cookie sheet and place waxed paper between layers. They may be cooked immediately or chilled up to 24 hours before cooking. (Or they may be frozen at this point for up to one week. Defrost in the refrigerator for 3 hours before cooking.)

To cook: Drop pasta into a large pot of boiling water and stir gently. Simmer for 2 to 3 minutes or until pasta is *al dente*–still firm but cooked through.

To serve hot: Remove pasta from water and toss with an herb butter.

To serve cold: Remove pasta from water and rinse in cold water to stop the cooking process. Toss with oil to prevent sticking. Add to chicken salad and toss with an herbal vinaigrette.

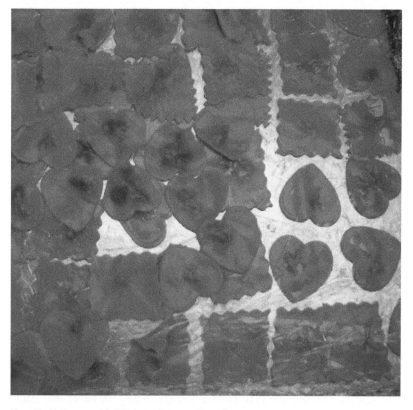

Egg Roll Pasta with Violets. *Donna Frawley*

Candied Leaves and Flowers

Candying fresh flowers is another way to preserve them for later use. There are several different ways to do this. Since it is no longer recommended that raw egg white be used, I use egg white powder or meringue powder. You can find meringue powder at Michaels or a cake supply store.

Candies 25 to 50 flowers

1/2 tablespoon meringue powder
1/2 to 1 teaspoon water
Super fine sugar in white or colored sugar to match flower color

Whisk together all ingredients. Let set for 15 minutes and whisk again. Paint mixture onto flowers and leaves with a small paint brush. Sprinkle with white or colored sugar. Set on waxed paper to dry.

When dry, store in an air-tight container. Use as a garnish on ice cream, cake, pudding, cookies, or any place a pretty flower might make a nice accent. Use flowers that complement a sweet dessert, like pansies, Johnny-jump-ups, lilacs, roses, or honeysuckle. They will keep from 2 weeks to one year.

Violet Syrup

Use violets, pansies, or Johnny-jump-ups. Lovely in tea breads, cupcakes, puddings, ices, fruit compotes, chilled soup, or poured over ice cream.

To retain color, do not allow the liquid to boil after flowers are added.

Makes about 1/2 to 3/4 cup syrup

2 ounces fresh violets
6 tablespoons water, boiling
1/2 cup sugar

Put flowers into glass jar. Pour boiling water over flowers, cover, and infuse for 24 hours. Strain. Add sugar and just heat to dissolve sugar.

Cool, bottle and refrigerate. Keeps in the refrigerator about one week or freeze for longer storage.

Pansy Sorbet

This was adapted from Jim Long's recipe "Spring Violets Sorbet" in his Fabulous Herb and Flower Sorbets—it is his recipe—except that I used fewer violets and added opal basil and lemon zest. I use an ice shaver, which has dishes that you freeze the mixture in, then put the frozen mixture into the ice shaving device and turn the handle to pass the mixture over the blade, to shave it like a "snow cone."

Makes 8 to 10 (1/2 cup) servings

1/2 cup sugar
3/4 cup dark purple violets or pansies, loosely packed, green calyxes removed
1/4 cup opal basil leaves
3 1/2 cups water
2 tablespoons freshly squeezed lemon juice
1 teaspoon lemon zest
Fresh violets, pansies, or Johnny-jump-ups for garnish

Place sugar, violets, and basil in a food processor and process until flowers and herbs are tiny bits of color in the sugar. Bring water to just boiling, remove from heat, add the flower/herb/sugar mixture and stir until sugar is dissolved.

Cover pan and let the mixture stand until it reaches room temperature (an hour or so). Pour liquid through a strainer and press with the back of a spoon, forcing the color out and into the liquid. Anything left in the strainer, discard. Stir in the lemon juice and lemon zest and chill mixture for an hour or two. Follow the manufacturer's instructions and freeze in a sorbet maker, ice cream freezer, or in ice shaver dishes.

Serve in chilled dishes and garnish with fresh flowers or an opal basil leaf.

Donna Frawley started her business in 1983 by selling at her local Farmers Market. Having majored in Home Economics and worked at a private country club, she used those skills to develop 60 culinary herb blends, 8 herb-flavored vinegars, and 8 herbal teas. She carries bulk culinary herbs and spices plus fresh herbs that are sold at LaLonde's Market and Eastman Party Store in Midland, Michigan. You can purchase her culinary mixes on her website: www.frawleysfineherbary.com.

Donna has written three books, *The Herbal Breads Cookbook, Our Favorite Recipes,* and *Edible Flowers Book.* She created the DVD *Cooking with Herbs* and writes a monthly herb column for her local newspaper and *Midland Neighbors* magazine. In March 2010 she had her first article published in the *Herb Companion.* She also writes a weekly e-newsletter; subscribe by going to Frawley's Fine Herbary FaceBook page.

Donna hosts cooking parties, teaches cooking classes and speaks on many culinary herb topics. She was a regular instructor at Whiting Forest in Midland, Michigan. Donna's non-fiction book, *Make a Difference*, is due out in 2022 and her historical fiction novel, *Weymouth Place,* set in Dubuque, Iowa, from 1860 to 1875, is due out in 2023.

Donna is a member of the Valley Herb society and the International Herb Association (IHA).

Violas ~ Valiant and Versatile

Cooper Murray

During these changing times, often fast-paced and stressful, we all long for a moment to unwind and enjoy nature. That said, the old saying "We eat first with our eyes," is the perfect phrase as we highlight violas.

As I create recipes to share, violas are never the main ingredient. They can be the *piece de resistance*, making the food more appealing and appetizing. Violas are not only a garnish. They bring an added depth to the recipe with their slightly grass-like and sometimes mint-like flavor.

My passion for cooking with herbs has developed as we celebrate violas. Having just built a home with my husband Paul on top of Green Mountain in Alabama, we are fortunate to have violas growing in the woods. These beautiful little flowers pop up in spring, sharing with us the splendor of nature as we enjoy walks with our dogs, Harriett and Wilson.

As an educational cooking motivator, I encourage you to step back, celebrate the beauty of food and be thankful for all that we have. Violas are the perfect example of an herb, with its qualities and grace.

Add a few violas to your recipes. They will bring you a taste of cheeriness.

Close up of Johnny-jump-up whiskers. *Susan Belsinger*

Viola Tea Sandwiches. *Cooper Murray*

Cucumber and Viola Tea Sandwiches with Herb Aioli

I have always enjoyed making different types of tea sandwiches. Something about these delicious little bites makes parties extraordinary. Fresh cucumbers that are small are the perfect size. The Herb Aioli for the tea sandwiches can be made ahead and kept in the refrigerator for up to 5 days.

Serves 8

Herb Aioli

1 1/2 cups mayonnaise
1 teaspoon chopped fresh dill
1 teaspoon chopped fresh parsley
2 teaspoons chopped fresh chives

In a small bowl, combine mayonnaise, dill, parsley, and chives. Mix until smooth. Cover and refrigerate.

Viola Tea Sandwiches

1/2 seedless cucumber or 3 small cucumbers
1/2 cup arugula, thinly sliced
16 slices thin-sliced rye or white bread, crusts removed
1/2 cup viola flowers, plus a few extra for garnishing the plate

Peel and thinly slice cucumber. Place between layers of paper towels to remove excess moisture. (This step can be done 1 day ahead.)

Spread each bread slice with Herb Aioli. Layer cucumber slices over aioli on 8 bread slices. Top with arugula. Sprinkle violas on top of the cucumbers. Top with remaining bread slices, aioli-side down.

Cut each sandwich into quarters, making a triangle. Serve on a platter or appetizer plates. Garnish with a few violas.

These can be made up to 1 hour ahead. If making prior to serving, cover with a slightly damp kitchen towel to keep sandwiches soft.

Massaged Kale and Viola Salad. *Cooper Murray*

Massaged Kale and Viola Salad

Salads are always a favorite, being both delicious and healthy. Kale salads are so popular, appearing everywhere on restaurant menus. Many friends tell me that they cannot eat kale raw, as it can be too tough and sometimes bitter. I introduced my massaged kale salad to them, changing their outlook. Massaging kale breaks down the fibers, which makes it easily digestible and softens the leaves. Violas, celery and parmesan cheese bring the lonely kale to the next level. As we used to say in the restaurant business "This recipe is money!"

For the dressing:
Juice of 1 lemon
1/4 teaspoon salt
1/4 teaspoon pepper
2 teaspoons honey (or coconut sugar)

1 bunch kale (curly kale works well)
1/4 cup olive oil
1/4 teaspoon salt
1/4 teaspoon pepper

2 stalks celery, thinly sliced
1/2 cup grated Parmesan cheese
1/2 cup viola flowers

Strip the kale from tough stems. Wash thoroughly and dry. Rough chop the kale into bite-size pieces and place it into a large bowl. Drizzle olive oil over the kale. Sprinkle with 1/4 teaspoon salt and 1/4 teaspoon pepper. Massage kale with oil for 2 to 3 minutes. The kale will decrease to about half the amount. Set the bowl aside while you prepare the dressing.

In a medium bowl, add lemon juice, salt, pepper, and honey, then whisk to blend the flavors.

Add celery, Parmesan cheese and dressing to kale, and mix well. Add half of the violas and lightly toss. Serve on individual plates or a platter. Garnish with remaining violas.

Viola and Orange-Infused Water. *Cooper Murray*

Viola and Orange-Infused Water

Catering is part of my business, and, to our guests' delight, we often serve refreshing herb-infused waters. Violas are no exception, adding health benefits and eye appeal.

Oranges are used in this recipe, although other fruits may be substituted with success. This water can be made in a large pitcher or a few large canning jars for fun.

Serves 4

1/2 cup violas
2 large oranges, sliced
1 gallon water
4 cups ice cubes

Gently wash the violas in a bowl of water. Place violas on paper towels to dry so that their color will be retained. Add orange slices and violas to a pitcher and add water. Cover with plastic and refrigerate for at least 6 hours

Serve over ice in glasses.

Easy to make festive party ice cubes—just place a violet in each section, add water and freeze. *Susan Belsinger*

Vichyssoise with Violas

Homemade soup is always welcome in our home. After inviting my mother-in-law for dinner, I decided to make vichyssoise. I had fresh potatoes from the farmers market and my violas were blooming.

As I shared my dinner idea with my husband, he questioned my selection. Was I up to this challenge? My mother-in-law is from France and is quite particular, especially when it comes to French cooking. Happily, "Maman" loved the vichyssoise. She had never had violas floating on this delightful soup. The violas were the perfect accompaniment. *Bon Appetit!*

Serves 6

4 tablespoons unsalted butter
6 leeks, white part only, cleaned and thinly sliced
2 large potatoes, cut into small cubes
1/4 teaspoon salt
1/4 teaspoon white pepper
4 cups chicken stock
2 cups heavy cream
Pinch of nutmeg
3 green onions, thinly sliced with scissors
1/4 cup violas

Heat the butter in a large pot over medium heat. Add the leeks and cook for 5 minutes until soft. Add the potatoes, salt and pepper and cook uncovered for a few minutes. Add chicken stock and bring to a boil. Reduce heat and simmer uncovered for 45 minutes, stirring occasionally.

Allow to cool for 1/2 hour on the stove. Place in the refrigerator for 1 hour. Remove from refrigerator and using an immersion blender, pulse until smooth. (A regular blender may be used, working in small batches).

Whisk in heavy cream and nutmeg. Stir in green onions. If you prefer a thinner soup, add more stock.

Cover with plastic and refrigerate at least 3 hours or overnight. Stir again before serving. Serve in soup bowls with 6 violas floating in the center.

Tamara "Cooper" Murray, BA, MA, is a graduate of Nazareth College and the University of Kansas. Originally from Binghamton, New York, and after living for many years in Colorado, she now calls Alabama her home and enjoys the long growing season of the South. Cooper's influence came from her grandmother who immigrated to the United States and became a cook in New York City. Cooper furthered her culinary knowledge working at country clubs and restaurants.

She creates recipes that highlight herbs and has written for numerous magazines and publications. Cooper's fondness for herbs and cooking led her to develop Organic Herbal Cooking, Inc. Her company offers motivational and educational cooking events in the southeast. She writes Organic Herbal Cooking's blog and shares the benefits of using herbs in simple, healthy cooking. Cooper is also the Special Events Director at Burritt on the Mountain, a living history museum in Huntsville, Alabama. She creates events to encourage visitors to experience Burritt. She loves herbs and usually any conversation with her leads to talking about fresh herbs! Not a day goes by that Cooper is not savoring the benefits of cooking with herbs.

Contact Cooper at organicherbalcooking.com or coopertmurray@gmail.com.

Spring roll with violets. *Deb Jolly*

Wild Violet Jelly. *Phyllis Williams*

Wild Violet Jelly

Phyllis Williams

Two or three years ago I was looking up information on wild violets and came across recipes for jelly, syrup, and such. I have a very large patch of *Viola sororia* in my yard, and I love making jelly, so I came up with my own jelly recipe. Serve with toast, breads, or crackers as you would use any jelly.

Yield: about 5 cups

2 cups wild violet flowers, lightly packed
2 cups water, boiling
2 tablespoons lemon juice
4 cups sugar
1 package Sure-Jell Fruit Pectin

Pick 2 cups wild violet flowers, lightly packed; place in a clean quart jar. Pour the 2 cups boiling water over the flowers, press to release any air bubbles and mash the flowers some. Cover the jar and place out of bright sunlight for 24 hours. The violet infusion will be a beautiful shade of blue.

When you're ready to make the jelly, line a colander with a coffee filter and strain the infusion. Make sure to press all the liquid from the flowers, to get the color and the essence. If needed, add enough water to make 2 cups liquid.

Measure lemon juice and sugar and have ready. Have the pectin ready to use, and have your jars clean, sterilized. and ready to fill.

In a deep pot, mix the infusion, lemon juice and pectin. Stir until pectin is dissolved and bring to a rolling boil. Jelly will need to be stirred constantly while cooking to prevent scorching. The jelly will turn a light lavender.

Add the sugar, stir in well and bring back to a rolling boil. Boil at least 1 minute; continue to stir constantly. For a test, drop a little jelly in a small bowl and let cool slightly, to make sure the jelly is ready to gel.

Pour into jelly jars, filling to bottom of rim. Wipe top rim of jars with a clean damp cloth, place sterilized lids on and tighten.

Place jars in water bath with 1 inch of water to cover and let come to a rolling boil for 1 minute. Remove jars from water bath and place out of draft to cool; check that all lids are sealed.

Jelly will keep up to 5 years. Enjoy!!!

Phyllis Williams lives outside Cave City, Arkansas, home of the World's Sweetest Watermelons, with her wonderful husband, David and dog, Bella. Phyllis and David attend church at Evening Shade First Baptist Church, where she leads a women's Bible study group and other activities. She is a retired home health nurse. She now is a Living History Interpreter at the Ozark Folk Center State Park at The Shannon Cabin Homestead.

Phyllis enjoys gardening and anything that has to do with herbs. She uses herbs in cooking, cleaning, crafts, and as medicinal remedies. She also loves hiking, looking at plants, and foraging for wild edibles, especially mushrooms. She likes finding and trying out new recipes using the wild plants that grow on their 10 acres.

Phyllis is Chair of the Herb Society of America-Ozark Unit, headquartered at the Ozark Folk Center. She is also a member of the Arkansas Fungi and Mushroom Association and the International Herb Association.

Wild violets. *Phyllis Williams*

Wild violet flowers gathered for jelly. *Phyllis Williams*

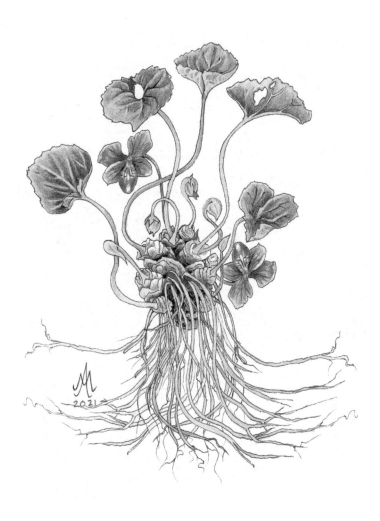

Alicia Mann

Healing & Beauty with Viola

Common blue violet, Stone County, Arkansas. *Deb Jolly*

Natural Beauty with Violas

Janice Cox

I always know spring is here when I see the sweet violets bloom around my yard. I never planted them; they just appear each year like a gift from Mother Nature. Cool, moist, and soothing is how I would describe this beautiful herb plant. I also grow violets, violas, pansies, and Johnny-jump-ups as an annual flower in my garden and containers. Some of them survive the winter if they are a bit protected, but it is the wild violets that I can depend on. Violets will spread each year and can also be started from seeds and stem cuttings. Plant them in the early spring, four to five inches apart and soon you will have your own sweet violet patch.

Violets, like many herbs, have been used since ancient times. They are mentioned in Greek history, where they were used in teas and baths for their soothing and cleansing properties. Violet water has long been a popular men's aftershave. It is slightly astringent and rich in vitamins A and C, both key ingredients for healthy skin. Violets are also mild enough to be used in children's products. Violet flower essential oil is difficult to make and expensive, much like rose oil. Most products use infused oils instead as the foundation for creating creams, lotions, and healing salves.

Infused violet oil is useful in treating minor scrapes, cuts, and insect bites. Its uses are similar to those of calendula or lavender oil. It is soothing and has anti-inflammatory properties. When making infused oils, it is important to only use dried plant material. You do not want to introduce any extra moisture that may cause bacteria to grow. For creating teas or tinctures that are water and alcohol based, using fresh or dried flowers and leaves works just fine. When I make infusions, I usually start with 1 tablespoon of dried plant material to 1 cup of what I wish to infuse (oil, sugar, honey, vinegar, alcohol). Then after the mixture sits for a few days, you can always add a bit more dried herbs for a stronger scent or dilute with your base.

I like to experiment with different infusions and see which ones I like best and want to use. Violets react very differently in different bases. In water they become almost colorless, but when vinegar is added they give the water a pretty pale pink tint. Have fun with your own tests; just make sure to keep notes so that you can recreate what combinations you prefer.

Drying viola flower petals and leaves is a simple process. You can make a drying tray out of some scrap wood and window screen or cover a cookie sheet with a cotton dishtowel to lay your herbs on. Harvesting in the morning works best. Clip off the flower heads and leaves. Rinse them with cool water and pat dry. Then lay them out on the drying tray. Place it in a warm spot but not in direct sunlight, and usually in a few days they should be dry. I store my flower heads and petals in glass jars in a dark cupboard to preserve their color and natural scent. You can also purchase tinted jars that block UV light; these are usually amber or blue in color. Some people use the oven, but I like the slow, old-fashioned method of air-drying, so that I don't have to worry about burning my herbs. I love to use the dried flowers in recipes or even as a "floral confetti" to add beauty to my morning oatmeal or fruit smoothie. A good rule of thumb is to use half the amount of dry to fresh herbs.

Here are a few of my favorite natural beauty recipes that you can create at home using violas, violets, and pansies. If you do not have any growing in your yard, do not worry; perhaps your neighbors have some or you can discover a wild patch in your area. Just make sure when foraging to ask permission, and make sure that the area you are picking from has not been sprayed with harmful chemicals. When picking in the wild, good etiquette is to only take what you really need and never pick more than one third of a plant. This will ensure that the plants will remain healthy and continue to grow and thrive. Enjoy!

Pat Kenny

Violet Water

Violet water is a classic skincare product that has been used since ancient times to treat and heal the skin. It is as easy to make as a cup of tea and can be used as a skin freshener, after-bath spray, or after-shave splash. I like to use a combination of fresh flowers and leaves, as I feel that both are rich in vitamins and healthy natural skincare ingredients like salicylic acid.

Yields 8 ounces

1/2 cup fresh violet flowers and leaves
1 cup boiling water
1/8 teaspoon vitamin E oil (optional but will extend the shelf life)

Place the flowers and leaves in a glass jar or ceramic bowl. Pour the boiling water over them and allow the mixture to cool completely. Strain the liquid into a clean container and discard the flowers and leaves. Stir in the vitamin E oil. To use: Splash or spray onto clean skin.

Violet Vinegar Toner

Natural vinegar such as apple cider or wine vinegar can be mixed with water and used as a toning spray or splash to restore your skin's natural pH after cleansing. Most cleansers or soaps are alkaline so they can alter the skin's natural acid mantle over time. Our skin needs a healthy dose of acid to help keep it clean and protected. Using floral waters not only makes the product smell good, but you also get the benefits of the herbs and flowers used. If you have dry or sensitive skin, double the amount of water called for.

Yields 4 ounces

1 tablespoon apple cider vinegar, wine vinegar or violet vinegar
1/2 cup violet water or strong violet tea
1 to 2 tablespoons rosewater

Mix together all ingredients and pour into a clean container with a tight-fitting lid. To use: Apply to clean skin after cleansing with a cotton pad. Rinse well with cool water.

Violet Cleansing Cream

Fresh violets give this cleansing cream recipe a wonderful delicate fragrance. You'll find it's a splendid treat for your skin. If you do not have access to fresh violets, you may substitute fresh pansies or dried violets.

Yields 4 ounces

1 tablespoon coconut oil
1/4 cup light natural oil such as almond, jojoba, or sunflower
1 to 2 teaspoons fresh violet flowers or 1/2 to 1 teaspoon dried
1/4 cup distilled water

Mix together the oils in a heat-resistant container. Heat until the oils begin to melt, remove from heat, and stir until melted and well mixed. In a separate bowl, mix together the violets and water. Heat this solution until just boiling. Pour the heated oil mixture into a blender and turn the blender on low. Slowly add the hot violet infusion and continue to blend. You will have a pale lavender-colored lotion. Let the cleansing lotion cool completely, then pour it into a clean container.

To use: Massage into your skin and rinse well with warm water.

Sweet Violet Flower Facial

A flower petal facial steam is a good way to deep cleanse your pores. The heat and humidity gently open your pores, allowing impurities to escape. Fresh violets and pansies create a fragrant facial steam that will keep your skin soft. They are also mildly astringent so even oily skin types can use this recipe. Please note: Steaming is not recommended for badly blemished skin. It can aggravate the condition by stimulating blood vessels and activating oil glands.

Yields one treatment

2 cups water
1/2 cup fresh violet flowers and leaves

Bring the water to a boil, remove from the heat, then add the flowers and leaves; stir. Let the mixture sit for 5 minutes. Lean over the pot, at least 12 inches from the surface and drape a towel over your head to form a tent. Close your eyes and let the steam rise over your face for 5 minutes. Rinse with cool water and pat dry.

Violet Vinegar Hair Rinse

Violet vinegar diluted in water makes a cleansing hair rinse for your scalp. Healthy hair comes from a healthy scalp. This rinse is soothing and mildly anti-inflammatory. When used weekly to keep your scalp conditioned and clear, you should notice an overall improvement in the condition of your hair.

Yields 8 ounces

1 tablespoon dried violet flowers or 2 tablespoons fresh
1 cup white vinegar or apple cider vinegar
1 cup water

In a clean jar or bowl, add the violets and pour the vinegar and water over them. Let the mixture sit for several hours or overnight. The vinegar will turn a lovely pink color. Strain and pour into a clean container. Discard the used flowers.

To use: Add 1 tablespoon of the violet vinegar water to one cup of water. After shampooing your hair, pour this rinse over your head and massage into your scalp. Rinse well with warm water. Note: Never use straight vinegar on your hair or skin.

Viola Combs and Brushes

Another nice way to enjoy your violas and treat your hair is by decorating a favorite brush or new wooden comb or brush with pressed flowers, leaves and petals.

Cut fresh flowers in the morning and make sure they are clean and dry. To flatten and press your botanicals, place them inside a large heavy book, sandwiched between parchment or wax paper. You can also purchase a flower press or make one using some wood scraps and screws. In a few weeks the flowers will be dry and ready to use. Using a waterproof decoupage glue or varnish, paint the surface of your comb or brush. Arrange your flowers and leaves in a pleasing pattern and let dry completely. When dry cover your entire design with two more coats of glue or varnish. These hair styling combs and brushes make a nice gift by themselves or combined with other homemade products and treats.

Ancient Viola Bath Soak

In ancient Greece, violet leaves and pansy flowers were used to create a relaxing bath soak that was believed to quiet the mind. Fresh violet leaves are rich in vitamin C and pansies contain salicylic acid, both key ingredients for healthy skin. For an indulgent touch you may want to scatter fresh flowers in your bathwater or place a small bouquet near your tub.

Yields 16 ounces, enough for one bath

1/2 cup fresh violet leaves
1/2 cup fresh pansy flowers
1 cup Epsom salts
1/2 cup baking soda
1 tablespoon natural oil such as light sesame, olive, or jojoba

In a small dish or bowl, mix together all the ingredients until well blended. Place inside a muslin tea bag or tie up in a cotton washcloth. As you fill the tub, place the bundle into the warm water and let the leaves, flowers, and salts scent and infuse your bathwater. Soak for 20 minutes.

Viola boudoir art. *Janice Cox*

Violet Body Powder

I remember my grandmother using body powder after bathing and she had the most beautiful blue powder puff made from ostrich feathers. Body powders keep your skin soothed and dry. They are especially useful during the summer months and help avoid skin conditions caused by heat rash. You can also sprinkle this softly scented powder on your sheets at night for sweet dreams.

Yields 4 ounces

1/2 cup corn flour or rice flour
1 tablespoon dried violet or pansy flowers

In a food processor or spice grinder, process the flour and dried flowers until you have a well-mixed powder. Spoon into a clean, dry container. To use: Sprinkle on your skin, clothing, or bed sheets.

Janice Cox is an expert on the topics of natural beauty and making your own cosmetic products with simple kitchen and garden ingredients. She is the author of six books on the topic: *Natural Beauty at Home, Natural Beauty for All Seasons, Natural Beauty from the Garden, Beautiful Luffa, Beautiful Lavender* and *Beautiful Flowers.* She is currently the beauty editor for *Herb Quarterly* and a speaker at *The Mother Earth News* fairs. Janice lives in Medford, Oregon, with her husband. She is a member of The Herb Society of America and International Herb Association.

Pat Kenny

The Medicinal Uses of Heartsease (*Viola tricolor*) [Violaceae]

Daniel Gagnon, Medical Herbalist RH (AHG)

Other Common Names:
English: European wild pansy; garden violet; Johnny jumper; Johnny-jump-up; pansy; stepmother; wild pansy; wild violet (Uphof 1968, Nickells 1976, Van Hellemont 1986, Bartram 1998 McGuffin 2000). In older English herbal books, heartsease was called *Herba Trinitaris*. It is believed that the plant was called by this name because each flower has three petal colors (Grieve 1971).

French: Pensée sauvage; violette des champs; violette tricolore; herbe de la Trinité (Valnet 1992).

German: Feldstiefmütterchen; ackerveilchen; stiefmütterchenkraut; dreifaltigkeitsblume; dreifarbiges veilchen (Van Hellemont 1986).
Italian: Pensiero (Van Hellemont 1986).
Spanish: Pensamiento (Wichtl 2004).

Part Used: Leaf and flower.

Herbal Properties: Authors have lauded heartsease's alterative, antiacne, antiallergic, anti-inflammatory, antioxidant, antirheumatic, demulcent, depurative (purifying), diuretic, emollient, expectorant, mild laxative, mucilaginous, pectoral (respiratory protective), and vulnerary (wound healing) properties (Nickells 1976, Bartram 1998, Skenderi 2003).

Constituents: The plant is rich in mucilage (approximately 10%). It also contains gums, saponins, copious amounts of flavonoids (including flavonols: rutin, quercetin, violanthin, vicenine 2, scoparine, scopoletin, luteolin, myricetin, orientin, and vitexin); phenolic acids (such as salicylic acids, gentisic acids, and caffeic acids); gaultherin, (a.k.a. methyl-salicylate); phenol glycosides (violutoside, etc.); tannins, carotenoids (such as violoxanthin), and coumarins). (Bartram 1998, Raynaud 2007, Skenderi 2003, Vukics 2008ª, Vukics 2008b).

When the plant, especially the root is bruised, the smell may remind you of a faint bitter almond odor (aka hydrogen cyanide) (Grieve 1971). Note that approximately 1 in 4 individuals possess a specific recessive genetic trait and are unable to detect the faint bitter almond smell from the bruised plant (Gidlow 2017).

Chew a heartsease leaf or flower and you'll experience a very pronounced taste of wintergreen. This is due to the presence of a constituent called methyl salicylate, the same compound found in wintergreen (*Gaultheria procumbens*) herb (Leclerc 1976).

Differentiating between Violas

Heartsease is an annual herb that is very widely distributed. It is found in Europe, including England; Asia; North and South America; as far north as the Arctic, Europe and western Siberia; as well as North Africa and Northwest India. It is cultivated in Holland and France. The herb found in commerce in Europe and the United States is most commonly sourced from Holland (Wichtl 2004).

Although there are numerous species of violets, they can be divided into two major categories; those whose flowers have three petals on top and two at the bottom (odorant violets) and those whose flowers have four petals on top and a single petal on the bottom (heartsease) (Mésségué 1975).

Two varieties of heartsease are known. The first one, *Viola tricolor* ssp. *arvensis*, is commonly called field pansy. It has small yellow or white flowers, and, as its name indicates, grows mainly in fields. The second one, *Viola tricolor* ssp. *vulgaris*, is commonly referred at to as ordinary wild pansy. This subspecies is larger and has violet flowers. It grows mainly in the grassland, which is referred to as "common land" in Europe, for the land that is shared by many people as a community resource. In Europe, both subspecies are used interchangeably in herbal medicine.

European herbalists have long insisted that it is important to include the word *tricolor* (*Viola tricolor*) when writing the prescription in Latin. This is done to prevent the pharmacist who is filling the prescription from confusing heartsease with sweet violet (*Viola odorata*), the root of which is often used as an expectorant. (Grieve 1971, Van Hellemont 1986, Weiss 1988).

For years, Ellen, my significant other, has planted heartsease and other annuals in the flowerpot closest to the main entrance of our home. The flowerpot is in a corner near the door, well protected from direct sunlight. In New Mexico, heartsease doesn't do well in direct hot sunlight; it soon wilts, dries, and dies. In partial shade, it continues to bloom late into the fall. After all the other plants have succumbed to frost, heartsease continues to thrive, sometimes as late as early December.

A Very Brief Herbal Medicine History of Heartsease

In Athens and Rome alike, heartsease's medicinal and mystical virtues were revered. Hippocrates (460-370 BCE), who is considered the father of medicine, recommended heartsease against headaches, the "vapors" of drunkenness, and various vision problems. He also recommended the herb for such conditions as melancholia, bile excess, and chest inflammation. During the Middle Ages, the herb was thought to be a remedy against cancer. During the same period Meshua, an Arab physician, prescribed it against constipation, angina, insomnia, and liver diseases. Over the years, its popularity rose when exalted by some writers and waned when its properties were deprecated by other writers (Mésségué 1975). However, through thick and thin, this herb became and remains an indispensable herb in herbal pharmacies throughout Europe and increasingly in North America.

The Medicinal Proprieties of Heartsease

Heartsease has been a staple of herbal medicine in Europe for centuries. In North America, it is becoming better known and continues to gain respect from herbalists who use it regularly. There are eight major medicinal areas where heartsease may benefit human health.

Heartsease and the Skin

Heartsease is best-known as an effective remedy for skin diseases. It is used both internally and externally for skin challenges such as eczema, acne, psoriasis, dandruff, itchiness, impetigo, ringworm, skin burns, skin eruptions, skin inflammation, skin ulceration, and urticaria (hives) as well as herpes outbreaks (Valnet 1992, Hoffmann 2003). For hundreds of years, it has been used for babies with cradle cap (seborrheic dermatitis) (Valnet 1992). In France, heartsease is known as a powerful *cicatrisante*, a plant that heals the skin (Raynaud 2007). Henri Leclerc (1976), a French medical doctor

(MD) and herbalist, prescribed it for skin diseases such as eczema, impetigo, psoriasis, milk crust (seborrheic dermatitis) in feeding infants, and juvenile acne. It is used in skin seborrheic states, often seen in conditions affecting the scalp, both internally as well as by local external applications (Schilcher 1997).

Externally, heartsease is used as a wash or wet compress for chronic skin disorders such as bacterial skin infections, common acne (i.e., acne vulgaris), dandruff, chronic eczema of internal origin, and milk crust. It has also been used as a sitz bath for vaginal irrigation, or as a wash for inflammation and itching of the vulvovaginal tissues (Skenderi 2003). Furthermore, studies have shown the herb's effectiveness externally on skin burns (Piana 2013[a], Piana 2013[b]).

Impetigo is a contagious skin infection commonly found in infants and young children. Over a period of about one week, the skin sores grow, burst, and develop a honey-colored crust. It is highly contagious and spreads rapidly among children who play together (*The Merck Manual* 1992). Heartsease has been shown to be highly effective for treating impetigo; it is recommended both internally and as an external skin wash to treat the affected skin area (Holmes 1989, Van Hellemont 1986). An in-vitro study has demonstrated the antimicrobial property of this herb against many bacteria, including *Staphylococcus aureus*, one of the main bacteria that causes impetigo (Witkowska-Banaszczak 2005). I can vouch that the results reported in treating impetigo with heartsease are credible, having witnessed them in my own practice.

Adults with chronic eczema respond well to heartsease when taken internally; however, it is necessary to continue with this therapy for some time, as one would expect with any chronic skin condition (Mésségué 1975). Some herbalists recommend heartsease specifically for eczema where there is much weeping (Hoffmann 1983). The treatment is simple. Use 2 teaspoons of the dried herb to a cup of boiling water, as an infusion. Drink one cup each morning and evening for several weeks. For infants with skin issues, it is best to use the infusion instead of water to prepare their food. This mild-tasting tea does not negatively affect the taste of the food (Weiss 1988).

English, French, and German herbalists have reported that heartsease combines well with other skin-specific plants such as burdock (*Arctium lappa*) root, cleavers (*Galium aparine*) herb, red clover (*Trifolium pratense*) blossom, stinging nettle (*Urtica dioica*) herb, and yellow dock *(Rumex crispus)* root (Hoffmann 1983, Weiss 1988, Bartram 1998, Raynaud 2007).

It is thought that heartsease's anti-inflammatory properties are due in large part to its constituents called saponins which have a cortisone-like effect. These anti-inflammatory properties may also be due to the phenolic acid constituents found in the herb, which have a NSAIDS-like effect (Skenderi 2003, Tolu 2007).

Heartsease and the digestive system

The leaves of heartsease are rich in a demulcent (soothing) substance called mucilage and are used against stomach or intestinal irritations of all kinds (Mésségué 1975). Heartsease has the reputation of being mildly laxative (Hoffmann 2003). It has also been used both internally as a tea and externally as compress against hemorrhoids (Valnet 1992).

Over the years, I have found that individuals with skin issues, such as eczema or psoriasis, tend to suffer from gastrointestinal issues. This GI irritation may be accompanied by diarrhea and constipation. By soothing the digestive system, heartsease offers much relief from skin problems. As the gastrointestinal tract inflammation recedes, the skin also begins to heal.

Combining heartsease with herbs such as dandelion (*Taraxacum officinalis*) root, calendula (*Calendula officinalis*) flowers, chickweed (*Stellaria media*) herb, red clover (*Trifolium pratense*) blossoms, and sarsaparilla (*Smilax ornata*) root will assist greatly in calming, soothing, and healing both the gastrointestinal tract and the skin (Menzies-Trull 2003). It's what I call a win-win for both organ systems.

Heartsease and the Urinary System

Heartsease has been recommended for diverse urinary health issues. For example, it is used for frequent and painful urination, especially when it is associated with such conditions as cystitis (Bartram 1998). The herbalist David Hoffmann (1983) suggests heartsease in combination with couchgrass (*Elymus repens*) rhizome and buchu (*Agathosma betulina*) leaf when treating cystitis, especially the recurrent type.

Some herbal medicine practitioners believe that supporting the urinary system helps to detoxify the skin, allay skin infections, and reduce skin eruptions (Menzies-Trull 2003). Part of the relief offered by heartsease may be due to the demulcent action of the herb on the urinary passages, the same action that soothes and calms the gastro-intestinal tract.

pastel hues beckon

johnny-jump-ups ease the heart

playful heartsease tease

Susan Belsinger

Heartsease, *Viola tricolor,* at Dow Gardens in Midland, Michigan.
Heather Cohen

Scurvy, Heartsease, Rutin, and the Cardiovascular System

Heartsease is an effective herbal medicine against bruising. It has been shown to stabilize and strengthen capillaries in all areas of the body. In order to make the connection between heartsease and healthy capillaries, allow me to digress.

For centuries, sailors from northern countries such as England and the Netherlands were very susceptible to a disease called scurvy. During their long voyages many of them would develop symptoms of anemia, tiredness, weakness, bone pain, easy bruising, tiny and large hemorrhages, bleeding gums, teeth loss, and swollen legs. Many of the untreated sailors would die. It was not uncommon for 25 to 50 percent of the crew to perish during long sailing trips. Navy physicians searched for solutions to this problem and observed that sailors suffered from scurvy because their diet was devoid of fresh foods. Some of the fresh foods that made the most difference in helping the sailors heal from their affliction included lemons, oranges, strawberries, blackberries, guava, kiwi fruits, papaya, tomatoes, carrots, sweet peppers, paprika, broccoli, potatoes, cabbage, spinach, liver, and oysters. Once sailors started eating these foods, they would heal from the dreaded disease. Finding a way to store fresh foods for long voyages remained a challenge for centuries.

In 1937, Albert Szent-Gyorgyi, a Hungarian biochemist and medical doctor, won the Nobel prize for physiology/medicine. Szent-Gyorgyi isolated and identified a compound he initially called hexuronic acid. He discovered that by giving adequate amounts of this substance to people with symptoms of scurvy, they would get better. A few years later he changed the name of hexuronic acid to ascorbic acid (aka Vitamin C) to better reflect what this substance did. In French, the word scurvy is "scorbut", while in Latin, the prefix "a" means without, thus ascorbic acid means "without scurvy". This is where the story gets interesting. When vitamin C is given to scurvy sufferers, all their symptoms disappear. However, bruising is a symptom that's difficult to overcome, even with vitamin C. Szent-Gyorgi further observed in his studies that ascorbic acid in fresh fruits and vegetables is intertwined with other nutrients called bioflavonoids. He isolated one specific flavonoid from fruits and found that this nutrient stopped capillary fragility more effectively than vitamin C (Crampton 1950). He first named the substance vitamin P (P for permeability). Later, he renamed it rutin. Science now fully recognizes that individuals who bruise easily are afflicted with capillary fragility and that rutin strengthens these weak capillaries.

Long before the discovery of vitamin C and rutin, herbalists had noticed that using heartsease flowers helped individuals who bruised easily. In the last few decades, we have learned that heartsease flowers are a very rich source of rutin (Turkoz 1995). In the *Handbook of Medicinal Herbs*, 2 ed., James Duke (2002) wrote that heartsease's edible flowers deliver a whopping 20 mg dose of rutin per gram of flowers. Although Duke retrieved the information on rutin and heartsease from the classic German medicinal herb text, *Hager's Handbuch*, he felt that this information should be verified. Dr. Duke would be happy to learn that the verification work has finally been completed. Recent research confirmed that heartsease contains approximately 33 mg of rutin per gram of flowers (Sofic 2010).

Heartsease's richness in rutin explains why it stabilizes and strengthens capillaries. When young and older individuals bruise easily, it often points to a deficiency of vitamin C AND rutin. The same capillary-strengthening properties of heartsease also help to check edema and prevent the buildup of fluids in tissues (Hoffmann 2003).

Corticosteroid therapy, used in asthma, allergic rhinitis, hay fever, hives, atopic eczema, chronic obstructive pulmonary disease (COPD), lupus, Crohn's disease, ulcerative colitis, polymyalgia rheumatica, and multiple sclerosis, is well known to weaken the capillaries and to lead to hemorrhages (Adkinson 2014). *The British Herbal Pharmacopoeia* (1983) suggests the use of heartsease to prevent capillary hemorrhage when a person is undergoing such therapy. The high quantity of rutin found in heartsease once again explains why it is so useful to prevent these treatment-induced side effects.

Heartsease is useful in the prevention or treatment of atherosclerosis. It has also been used as a heart tonic for many centuries. In association with other herbs like garlic (*Allium sativum*) bulb, linden (*Tilia cordata*) flower, dandelion (*Taraxacum officinale*) leaf, and passionflower (*Passiflora incarnata*) herb, it is used to reduce high blood pressure and address atherosclerosis challenges (Hoffmann 2003).

Heartsease flowers are considered to make an excellent cordial (a medicine that strengthens the heart) (Mitchell 2003). It is thought that it is this cardiovascular-strengthening action that helped the plant acquire the name heartsease. However, other writers believe that heartsease acquired its name because the herb was used alone or with other herbs as a love potion (Grieve 1971).

Heartsease and Joint Health

Heartsease has been used for centuries against arthritis and rheumatism (Hoffmann 2003). This is not surprising since the herb is rich in salicylates, quercetin, and rutin, three naturally occurring compounds that possess strong anti-inflammatory properties (Skenderi 2003). In Belgium, medical herbalists also recommend this herb for gout (Van Hellemont 1986). Research has shown that the tincture of heartsease possesses significant anti-inflammatory properties and is as effective as the anti-inflammatory drug diclofenac (Tolu 2007). Heartsease can be used to relieve pain, swelling (inflammation), and joint stiffness caused by arthritis. It is often combined with other herbs that address joint issues, such as black cohosh (*Actaea racemosa*) root, devil's claw (*Harpagophytum procumbens*) root, meadowsweet (*Filipendula ulmaria*) herb, pipsissewa (*Chimaphila umbellata*) herb, and willow (*Salix alba*) bark (Hoffmann 1983, Valnet 1992, Weiss 1988). It is important to remember that when addressing a long-standing problem such as joint disease, a person should continue using the herbal treatment for at least two or three months before deciding if it is helping. In the majority of cases, the health issue has been present for many years before the person started taking herbs. Give heartsease and other herbs the time to work their magic.

Heartsease and the Respiratory System

Saponins, a group of constituents found in heartsease, in part explain why the herb has been recommended as an effective expectorant. Another constituent called mucilage helps to soothe the throat and chest. That's why heartsease has been recommended to treat respiratory disorders such as whooping cough in children and acute bronchitis, pleurisy, as well as asthma in children and adults alike (Grieve 1971, Hoffmann 2003).

A tea made from a mixture of seven medicinal herb flowers is renowned in France as an excellent "pectoral tea" or "chest tea." This pectoral tea contains equal parts of field poppy (*Papaver rhoeas*) flower, mallow (*Malva sylvestre*) flower, marshmallow (*Althaea officinalis*) flower, pussytoes (*Gnaphalium dioicum*) flower, coltsfoot (*Tussilago farfara*) flower, mullein (*Verbascum thapsus*) flower as well as heartsease (*Viola tricolor*) flower. This formulation is reputed to possess substantial chest bronchial soothing properties and helps to relieve coughs, colds, bronchitis, pneumonia, and other respiratory issues (Mésségué 1975). You can find this or similar formulas in French pharmacies. A clinical trial in children with asthma using a heartsease syrup found that it helped to control dry irritable cough in conjunction with prescribed medication for asthma (Chevallier 2016).

Heartsease as a Possible Cancer Treatment

The literature surrounding heartsease is peppered with references on the use of this herb for cancer.

French herbal medicine books report the story of a man who "cured" his throat cancer with heartsease infusions and compresses. These herbalists suggested that heartsease may have stimulated his immune system and thus vanquished the cancer (Mésségué 1975, Valnet 1992).

Recent research suggests that heartsease has significant anticancer potential (Lindholm 2002, Svangard 2004, Mortazavian 2012, Sadeghnia 2014). It is thought that heartsease may be helpful in treating cancer as it seems to promote programmed cell death, a biological phenomenon whereby cells that are damaged beyond repair commit suicide. Science calls this phenomenon apoptosis. It's an important way our body prevents the growth and proliferation of cancer cells. A second way that heartsease shows potential anticancer potential is by inhibiting uncontrolled blood vessel growth. Angiogenesis is the process by which cancers encourage the growth of blood vessels to nourish its own unrestrained growth (Sadeghnia 2014).

In 2012, a laboratory study was conducted using different extracts of heartsease against cervix carcinoma cells in vitro. The research showed that the water and alcohol extract of the herb possessed potent inhibitory effects against the proliferation of these cancerous cells (Mortazavian 2012).

An extract of heartsease was separated into different fractions and these fractions were used in a laboratory study against human lymphoma cell and human myeloma cell. Three compounds showed excellent results against these cancerous cells. The researchers concluded that the potencies of these three compounds were in the range of the clinically used anticancer drug doxorubicin (Svangard 2004).

In Traditional Chinese Medicine (TCM), a relative of heartsease, *Viola patrinii* (Bliss 1973), has been researched for its usefulness against cancer (Roi 1955). Another Viola (*Viola yedoensis*) is being used in TCM to clear heat and eliminate toxins (Chen 2001). This herb is currently being investigated as an anti-metastatic treatment, specifically in lung cancer. In the most recent study, the researchers concluded that this herb may inhibit tumor invasion by suppressing the activity of certain enzymes in lung cancer cells (Huang 2018).

Obviously, it would be irresponsible to suggest that a person with cancer should use heartsease or other *Violas* as a primary treatment modality against this serious and treacherous disease. More research needs to be conducted to find the exact mechanisms of heartsease's action against cancer cells and how it works inside the human body. However, I would not hesitate to include a couple of cups of heartsease tea daily to put more chances on my side.

Harvesting Heartsease

Harvest heartsease early in the morning as soon as the dew evaporates. Only harvest the leaves and flowers. Do not bunch the herbs in a pile but spread them evenly in thin layers so they can dry quickly. Dry them in the shade as this will preserve the lovely color and smell of the flowers. Keep in closed paper bags away from humidity and light (Mésségué 1975).

How to Use Heartsease as a Medicine

Internally: Make a tea from the dried or fresh leaves and flowers; 2 full teaspoons (2 to 4 grams) to each cup of boiling water; let it sit/infuse for 15 minutes, covered. Filter. Use 1 cup two to three times a day (Bartram 1998). Herbal extract made with 70% alcohol (ethanol): Take 20 to 30 drops three times a day (morning, noon, and night) with meals (Raynaud 2007). Tablets/capsules: Two 250 mg (Bartram 1998).

In almost all cases, follow this regimen for at least one month and continue when results are encouraging (Bartram 1998).

Externally: Infuse 4 grams of the herb per cup of hot water for 10 minutes. Use as a compress in case of scalp seborrheic issues (cradle cap) in children (Raynaud 2007). Also use as a compress for skin diseases of all kinds, as well as hemorrhoids (Valnet 1992).
Safety: There are no safety concerns surrounding the use of this herb. The *Botanical Safety Handbook*, 2 ed. classifies heartsease as a Class 1 herb, an herb that can be safely consumed when used appropriately (Gardner 2013).
Contraindications: No contraindications are known for this herb (Gardner 2013).
Side Effects: This herb is known to give the urine the "smell of cat pee" (Valnet 1992).
Drug Interactions: The *Botanical Safety Handbook,* 2 ed. has classified heartsease as a Class A herb, an herb for which no clinically relevant interactions are expected (Gardner 2013).

References

Adkinson, NF., Bochner, BS., Burks, AW., Busse, WW., Holgate, ST., Lemanske, RF., O'Hehir, RE. *Middleton's Allergy Principles and Practice.* Elsevier Saunders, 2014.

Bartram, T. *Bartram's Encyclopedia of Herbal Medicine.* Constable and Robinson Ltd, 1998.

Bliss, B. *Chinese Medicinal Herbs.* Georgetown Press, 1973.

The British Herbal Pharmacopeia. British Herbal Medical Association, 1983.

Chen J, and T. Chen. *Chinese Medical Herbology and Pharmacology.* Art of Medicine Press, Inc., 2001.

Chevallier, A. *Encyclopedia of Herbal Medicine.* 3 ed. Dorling Kindersley Limited, 2016.

Crampton, EA and Lloyd, ED. "A quantitative estimation of the effect of rutin on the biological potency of vitamin C." *The Journal of Nutrition,* 1950. 41(3): 487-498.

Duke, J. *Handbook of Medicinal Herbs,* 2 ed. CRC Press, 2002.

Gardner, Z. and McGuffin, M. editors. *Botanical Safety Handbook,* 2 ed. CRC Press, 2013.

Gidlow, D. "Hydrogen cyanide – an update." *Occupational Medicine.* 2017. 67: 662-663.

Grieve, M. *A Modern Herbal.* Dover Publications, Inc., 1971. (reprint of 1931 ed.).

Holmes, P. *The Energetic of Western Herbs.* Artemis Press, 1989.

Hoffmann, D. *The New Holistic Herbal.* Element Books Limited, 1983.

Hoffmann, D. *Medical Herbalism.* Healing Arts Press, 2003.

Huang, SF., Chu, SC., Hsieh, YH., Chen, PN., Hsieh, YS. "*Viola yedoensis* suppresses cell invasion by targeting the protease and NF-kB activities in A546 and Lewis lung carcinoma cells." *International Journal of Medical Sciences.* 2018. 15(4) : 280-290.

Leclerc, H. *Précis de phytothérapie.* Masson, 1976.

Lindholm, P., Gorasson, U., Johansson, S., Claeson, P., Gullbo, J., Larsson, R., Bohlin, L. and Backlund, A. "Cyclotides: A novel type of cytotoxic agents." *Molecular Cancer Therapeutics,* 2002. 1: 365-369.

McGuffin, M., Kartesz, J.F., Leung, AY. and Tucker, A.O. *Herbs of Commerce*, 2 ed. American Herbal Products Association, 2000.

Menzies-Trull, C. *Herbal Medicine, Keys to Physiomedicalism including Pharmacopoeia*. Faculty of Physiomedical Herbal Medicine, 2003.

Mésségué, *M. Mon herbier de santé*. Laffont, 1975.

Mitchell, W. *Plant Medicine in Practice*. Elsevier Science, 2003.

Mortazavian, SM., Ghorbani, A., Hesari, TG. "Effect of hydro-alcoholic extracts of *Viola tricolor* and its fractions on proliferation of cervix carcinoma cells." *The Iranian Journal of Obstetrics, Gynecology and Infertility*, 2012. 15(22): 9-16.

Nickell, JM. *J.M. Nickell's Botanical Ready Reference*. CSA Press, 1976.

Piana, M., Zadra, Z., Faccim de Brum, T., Boligon, AR., Kieling Gonc,, AF., Corrê a da Cruz, R., Borba de Freitas, R., Scotti do Canto, G., Athayde, ML. "Analysis of Rutin in the Extract and Gel of *Viola tricolor*." *Journal of Chromatographic Science*, 2013a. 51: 406–411.

Piana, M., Silva, MA., Trevisan, G., Faccim de Brum, T., Silva, CR., Boligon, AR., Oliveira, SM., Zadra, M.. Hoffmeister, C., Rossato, MF., Tonello, R., Laporta, LV., Borba de Freitas, R., Belke, BV., Jesus, RS., Ferreira, J., Athayde. ML. "Antiinflammatory effects of *Viola tricolor* gel in a model of sunburn in rats and the gel stability study." *Journal of Ethnopharmacology*, 2013b . 150(2): 458-465.

Raynaud, J. *Prescriptions et conseils en phytothérapie*. Lavoisier, 2013b

Roi, J. *Traité des plantes médicinales chinoises*. Édition Paul Lechevalier, 1955.

Sadeghnia, HR., Hesari, TG., Mortazavia, SM., Mousavi, SH., Najaran, ZT., Ghorbani, A. "*Viola tricolor* Induces Apoptosis in Cancer Cells and Exhibits Antiangiogenic Activity on Chicken Chorioallantoic Membrane." *BioMed Research International*, Volume 2014, Article ID 625782, 8 pages.

Schilcher, H. P*hytotherapy in Paediatrics*. Medpharm Scientific Publishers, 1997.

Skenderi, G. *Herbal Vade Mecum*. Herbacy Press, 2003.

Sofic, E., Copra-Janicijevic, A., Salihovic, M., Tarihovic, I. and Kroyer, G. "Screening of medicinal plant extracts for quercetin-3-rutinoside (rutin) in Bosnia and Herzegovina." *Medicinal Plants*, 2010. 2(2): 97-102.

Svangard, E. Gorassan, U., Hocaoglu, Z. Gullbo, J., Larsson, R., Claeson, P., Bohlin, L. "Citotoxic cyclotides from *Viola arvensis*." *J. Nat. Prod.*, 2004. 67: 144-147.

The Merck Manual. 16 ed. Merck and Co., Inc, 1992.

Tolu, A., Parvu, AE., Oniga, I., Tamas, M. "Evaluation of anti-inflammatory activity of alcoholic extract from *Viola tricolor.*" *Revista Medico-chirurgicala a Societatii de Medici si Naturalisti din Iasi.* 2007. 111(2) 525-529.

Turkoz, S., Toker, G., Sener, B. "Investigation of some Turkish plants regarding of rutin." *J Fac Pharm Gazi.* 1995. 12(1): 17-21.

Uphof, J.C. *Dictionary of Economic Plants.* Stechert-Harner Service Agency, Inc., 1968.

Valnet, J. *Phytothérapie.* 6 ed. Maloine, 1992.

Van Hellemont, J. *Compendium de Phytothérapie.* Association Pharmaceutique Belge, 1986.

Vukics, V., Kery, A., Guttman, A. "Analysis of polar antioxidants in heartsease (*Viola tricolor* L.) and Garden Pansy (*Viola x wittrockiana* Gams.)." *Journal of Chromatographic Science.* 2008[a]. 46. 823-827.

Vukics, V., Toth, B.H., Ringer, T., Ludanyi, K., Kery, A., Bonn, G.K. "Quantitative and qualitative investigation of the main flavonoids in heartsease (*Viola tricolor* L.)." *Journal of Chromatographic Science,* 2008[b].46: 97–101.

Weiss, R. *Herbal Medicine.* Beaconsfield Publishers Ltd, 1988.

Wichtl, M. (Ed.) *Herbal Drugs and Phytopharmaceuticals.* 3 ed. CRC Press, 2004.

Witkowska-Banaszczak, E., Bulka, W., Matlawaska, I., Goslinska, O. Muszynski, Z. "Antimicrobial activity of *Viola tricolor* herb." *Fitotherapia.* 2005.76: 458-461.

Daniel Gagnon, Medical Herbalist, MS, RH (AHG) is a French-Canadian originally from Ontario who relocated to Santa Fe, NM in 1979. He has been a practicing Medical Herbalist since 1976. Daniel is the author of *The Practical Guide to Herbal Medicines*, a book designed to provide herbal health care options. With Amadea Morningstar, he is also the co-author of *Breathe Free*, a book on healing the respiratory system. He regularly teaches herbal therapeutics both nationally and internationally. Daniel is the owner of Herbs, Etc., an herbal medicine retail store and manufacturing facility. www. herbsetc.com. Daniel can be reached at botandan@aol.com.

Just-harvested violets ready for infusion. *Susan Belsinger*

I Love Violet Medicine!

Carol Little

Do you have a favourite spring/early summer bloom? Violets are definitely one of mine, especially Common/Sweet/Wood/ Blue Violets (*Viola odorata/V. sororia*). There is something so cheerful about these sweet little blossoms, peeking out from under their glossy, oh so green foliage. I have some plants who found their way into my garden, many years ago, and are still with me, growing each spring, back again and thriving. Most flowers of the violet family are edible. In fact, both the flowers and the leaves are wonderful mixed with other greens for a delicious salad. There are over 400 members of the violet family (Violaceae) and violet medicine is a powerful ally.

The delicate scent of these sweet flowers makes me think of days gone by, when it was quite normal to have violet tea as a part of a traditional High Tea. I love to enjoy fresh leaves and flowers when in season, and dry extra leaves for a lovely tea year-round. For optimum flavour and therapeutic value, harvest violet flowers mid-morning, after the dew has evaporated and before the hot sun wilts them.

Violets make me think of hope and optimism. When flowers are just beginning to pop up, I pick some every day and make an infused oil to use in breast cream or salves, a violet-infused vinegar to enhance summer salads, and a delightful violet syrup.

According to respected herbalist and one of my beloved teachers, Michael Vertolli, harvest both leaves and flowers from the top 25% of the plant. For every 2 to 3 flowers, use 1 leaf to create the mixture for tincturing.

The most important medicinal attributes of violets: anti-bacterial, anti-catarrhal, anti-inflammatory, anti-rheumatic, aperient, demulcent, diaphoretic (mild), diuretic, expectorant, lymphatic, nervine, relaxant, vasodilator, and vulnerary.
Violet medicine can be used for all types of coughs as it is soothing and

relaxing and loosens mucus. A good lung herb, violet is excellent for lower respiratory tract conditions. Violets are an excellent choice for toxicity-related conditions. As a lymphatic herb, they can ease congestion and calm inflamed lymph nodes. Violets are a deep-acting medicine and combine well in formulae. I also make violet tincture for my apothecary, as both violet flower and leaf have healing qualities. I like to add it to a formula that helps folks who need a lift, with lemon balm and lavender.

Violet Oil

I use infused oil of violet in combination with dandelion oil for making a lovely nourishing breast cream. Violet infused oil makes a delightful salve as well.

Materials you will need

Fresh-picked violets
Clean glass canning jars with tight-fitting lids
Good quality olive oil
Cheesecloth or muslin
Labels and marker

Place the violets in a glass jar. Top with a small amount of good quality olive oil. If you have a limited amount of harvest, put a lid on the jar and store until the following day, then add more flowers. Always cover the flowers with oil and keep the lid on the jar when not harvesting. Place the jar in a sunny place and let it steep for 2 weeks. Strain the oil using cheesecloth or muslin into a second glass jar. Gather up the cheesecloth and wring tightly to extract as much of the precious oil as possible. Cover, label, date, and store in a dark cupboard.

Note: If strained well, and stored well, the oil should be potent for 6 to 8 months. (I do have oils that are older and are just fine, but it's a good idea to have a plan for our infused oils.)

Violet Vinegar

Add some vitamins A and C to your meals. Any vinegar can be used to infuse violets, but the best results can be found when using a clear vinegar so that the gorgeous purple tints of the flowers have a chance to shine!

Add violets to a clean glass jar. Cover the violets with vinegar. Use white wine vinegar or white balsamic to maximize the glorious pink/mauve goodness from the infusion. I understand, from friends who also make this vinegar, that champagne vinegar works very well too. It is delightful!

Violet Tea

Add 2 to 3 teaspoons of fresh violet flowers to each cup of just boiled water. Allow to steep for five or six minutes, strain and serve.

Gorgeous Spring Violet Syrup

Who doesn't love making herbal syrups? If you haven't made these fun concoctions, syrups are an easy project and great fun for adults and kids alike. Violet syrup is decadent drizzled over vanilla ice cream or in a cocktail! The colour of your syrup will depend on the violet hue of your violets and the pH of your water. I have played with the colour with the addition of lemon juice. Just try a couple of drops and add a little more if you want a deeper purple tint.

Yields about 3 cups

2 cups fresh violet flowers
2 cups just-boiled water
2 cups honey (or sugar)
Lemon juice, optional

Place the violet flowers in a clean glass jar. Fill the jar with just-boiled water. Stir well. Cover. After 45 minutes, the water should be a beautiful violet colour. Allow to steep until the flowers have given up their colour. Strain and compost the violets.

Measure your violet-infused water and then measure an equal amount of your sweetener of choice. Add a few drops of lemon juice, if desired. Stir well. This 1:1 ratio will allow the syrup to store well in the fridge for up to six months. If you prefer a syrup which is not as sweet, just use less sweetener, but remember that it should be stored in the fridge and used within a month. Choose a glass container with a tight-fitting lid.

Violet Medicine in the Kitchen

Eat both the flowers and the leaves in your spring salads. Delicious. Use a violet-infused vinegar as a part of your vinaigrette. Add violet greens to a mixture of other steamed greens. Herbalist Susun Weed suggests that we can increase our calcium intake by enjoying a splash of vinegar on our greens.

Violet syrup can elevate your next spring dessert. Drizzle a little over a frozen treat or a fruit-topped shortcake. Use your imagination.

Enjoy violet medicine every way you can. Cultivated or ethically wild-harvested, violets are a wonderful part of spring!

References

Class notes from lectures by Michael Vertolli R.H. Living Earth School of Herbalism. 1998-2001.

Class notes from lectures by Rosemary Gladstar. Sage Mountain: The Science & Art of Herbalism apprenticeship. 1997.

Carol Little, R.H. is a traditional herbalist in Toronto, Canada, where she has had a private practice for the last 20+ years. She loves to write about how we can embrace herbs in our daily lives. Her easy-to-digest weekly blog posts offer quick takeaway ideas to help readers to feel their best. Come for a visit: https://www.studiobotanica.com. Check out her active Facebook community at https://www.facebook.com/studiobotanica and follow her on Instagram https://instagram.com/studiobotanica.

Carol is a current professional and past board member of the Ontario Herbalists Association. She combines her love of travel and passion for all things green and loves to write about both. Carol has written for *Vitality Magazine* for many years. She is a regular contributor to the IHA annual Herb of the Year book. She is a proud participant in the recently published *FIRE CIDER 101 Zesty Recipes for Health-Boosting Remedies* by Rosemary Gladstar and friends.

Purple violet blossoms. *Deb Jolly*

Viola odorata, Fragrance Specialty Garden, National Herb Garden. *Pat Kenny*

Science Supports *Viola*'s Traditional Medicinal Value

Dorene Petersen and Glen Nagel

Exquisite wild violet (*Viola odorata* L.) flowers fluttering in a gentle wind, like small, purple butterflies never fail to delight. Equally delightful is embarking on an exploratory journey, unearthing recent scientific studies, research reviews, and ancient texts that shed light on the constituents and the medicinal uses of *Viola odorata* (also abbreviated as *V. odorata*). This includes many that substantiate the traditional uses. The journey reveals a wealth of benefits through a historical and geographical landscape, from ancient Persian-Greek traditional medicine, known as Unaani, to Nicholas Culpeper (1616-1654),[1] global pharmacopoeias, to recent research published in Pubmed, Science Direct, and the Cochrane library

From the family Violaceae the two main medicinal species mentioned in literature and research are *V. odorata*[2] and *Viola tricolor* L. subsp. *curtisii* (E. Forst.) Syme.[3]

Viola odorata traditionally has been used since the time of the Greek physicians Asclepius (8th century B.C.) and Hippocrates (460 B.C. to 375 B.C.).[4] Many of the early uses that Culpepper discusses were said to be heavily influenced by the ideas of Paracelsus von Hohenheim (1493–1541) and followed the theory of the Doctrine of Signatures. At the time of Paracelsus, this doctrine was a useful evaluation tool that associated the plant's shape to medicinal uses. Unscientific but intriguing, nonetheless. Given that the leaf of the violet does have a shape that could at a stretch be a lung, the Doctrine of Signatures may have indeed influenced Culpepper's statement that "… the fresh or dried flowers and leaves are beneficial for pleurisy and all lung diseases, to lenify the sharpness of hot rheums and the hoarseness of the throat."

Similar uses of *V. odorata* leaves, flowers and roots in many forms from powders, pills, extracts, to syrups are recorded in the traditional medicine texts of Persia and Iran. The Persian physician Ibn-Sīnā, also known as Avicenna (ca. 970–1037), wrote about the virtues of violets.[5] It was known as a plant with a cold and wet temperament and has been used for hot and dry diseases such as fever, excessive thirst, and uremic pruritus. It also was widely recommended in Iranian traditional medicine for pulmonary diseases such as cough, pneumonia, and pleurisy.[6]

The Chemistry of *Viola odorata*

A 2017 review paper examines more closely the chemical composition and medical use of *V. odorata*. Ancient Persian texts as well as a complete review of electronic databases reveals 22 relevant studies, including three human studies and 16 *in vitro* studies up to 2017.[7]

The plant's chemistry represents a diverse array of chemical constituents. The flowers contain an essential oil, a blue pigment, as well as monoterpenes and sesquiterpenes including linalool, benzyl alcohol, cadinol, globulol, viridiflorol, sugar and a trace amount of melatonin. The leaves also contain an essential oil along with quercetin and salicylic acid, flavonoids, tannins, alkaloids such as violin (also found in the roots), and saponins. Two other studies state that the plant peptides (cyclotides), including cycloviolacin-O2 found in *V. odorata* show therapeutic potential.[8] [9] Further, a 2010 study demonstrated that cyclotide cycloviolacin-O2 from *V. odorata* has potent bactericidal activity against Gram-negative bacteria, further adding to its remarkable therapeutic repertoire. This is particularly good news given that Gram-negative bacteria are resistant to treatment with many antibiotics, and even botanical or essential oil treatments.[10]

A water extract of another member of Violacea, the European wild pansy or heart's ease, *V. tricolor,* also is a source of bioactive cyclotides which inhibit proliferation of activated lymphocytes and provide support for disorders related to an overactive immune system. Further studies to evaluate its clinical potency would need to be performed but the immunologic effects and anti-inflammatory action reveal *V. tricolor's* medicinal potential.[11]

Further, it is not a surprise, given the common name of heart's ease, that there is interest in using *V. tricolor* as a cardioprotective agent. Both *in vitro* and animal research has demonstrated that *V. tricolor* extracts have vasorelaxant and hypotensive effects. A 2020 *in vitro* animal study using the whole plant fluid extract of *V. tricolor* showed vasodilator, cardio-depressant, and anti-hypertensive effects. While the precise cardioprotective mechanism is still unclear, high performance liquid chromatography revealed the presence of gallic acid which has a potential role in cardiovascular diseases. Hence, *in vitro* and *in vivo* studies show the potential role of *V. tricolor* in treatment of cardiovascular diseases.

Viola odorata Medicinal Uses

Traditional Persian medicine has numerous mentions of the value of *V. odorata* for central nervous system problems such as insomnia, epilepsy, headache, nasal ulcers, and fevers. Also mentioned are cardiovascular conditions such as palpitations and tachycardia, along with respiratory conditions such as chronic lung problems, coughs, common colds, and pneumonia. [12] Interestingly, the British Pharmacopoeia also lists violet leaf *V. odorata folium* as an expectorant.[13] Urinary tract issues such as fluid retention, painful or difficult urination, and flank pain also were mentioned as ailments that responded to *V. odorata*. The authors of the review thought this action was due to the presence of flavonoids in *V. odorata*. The most reported route of administration, however, was topical. Topical powders and poultices were used for skin conditions, inflammation, stomach, and liver disease and even anal swelling, apparently in recent times often misdiagnosed as hemorrhoids. [14] Additionally, the research review revealed evidence of treatment of cancerous or malignant tumors and chronic inflammation.[15] Avicenna and Culpepper both mention many of the ailments above as being effectively treated by the humble but impactful *V. odorata*.

In support of the traditional belief that *V. odorata* has potential for respiratory conditions, a 2015 study addressed the growing problem of asthma in children and the need to find alternatives to traditional drug treatments. Researchers aimed to investigate the effect of violet syrup on cough alleviation in children with intermittent asthma. The results reinforced Culpepper's and Avicenna's writings. In this human, double-blind, placebo-controlled study, the authors demonstrated the effectiveness of a *V. odorata* flower syrup on the cough of children with intermittent asthma. The study enrolled 182 children between the ages of 2 and 12 all with intermittent asthma. They were randomized in a group receiving either violet flower syrup or placebo. Each group used no other medicine except for treatment with short-acting bronchodilators. The children in each group were evaluated in terms of the duration until 50% cough reduction and 100% cough suppression were achieved. The *V. odorata* cough syrup was composed of dried viola flowers, 12 grams per 100 cc. Each child received 2.5 cc or 5 cc, 3 times a day for 5 days.[16] The results from each group revealed no significant difference in cough reduction based on sex, age, place of living, and educational status of parents. Significant results showed the duration required to yield more than 50% cough reduction and 100% cough suppression was significantly less in the violet syrup group compared to placebo groups (statistically highly significant P<.001). There was significantly less wheezing occurrence in pulmonary examinations after the intervention in the violet syrup group than in the placebo group (also statistically highly significant).

This human study supports the long history of *V. odorata* flower syrups being used for coughs and upper respiratory mucus. Previously studies focused on the respiratory tracts of mice, which revealed that *V. odorata* flowers were anti-inflammatory and anti-asthmatic as well as effective in inhibiting the total serum levels of IgE and pro-inflammatory cytokines such as IL-3 and IL-4. Cytokines synchronize immune system responses to disease, in this case serving an anti-inflammatory function. This use of the syrup effectively decreased response of the airways and decreased eosinophilia, which are the body's white cells that attack disease and excessive mucus.

The researchers concluded that viola flower syrup is a potential natural cough suppressing treatment for children with intermittent asthma. They recommended that studies continue with larger sample sizes and other dosages to confirm the results of this study and select the best dosage.[17]

Culpepper mentions the efficacy of *V. odorata* for the "heat and sharpness of urine"[18] and, while not directly related, one of the challenges of late-stage kidney disease is treating a condition called uremic pruritus. Uremic pruritus, also known as "chronic kidney disease-associated pruritus" (CKD-aP), is chronic itching that occurs with patients who have advanced or end-stage renal disease.[19] It is known to affect about 20% to 50% of patients with renal failure and often causes long-term pain and suffering.[20] A 2019 study[21] concluded that the efficacy of treatment of hemodialysis pruritus with an infused oil of *V. odorata* flowers was more effective than just massage alone. The oil was formulated using fresh flowers in sweet almond oil in a ratio of 1-part oil to 1-part flowers. This was prepared in an incubator at 37 degrees Celsius (98.6° F). The final violet oil was standardized by optical absorption for gallic acid, revealing 27.6 mg/l of gallic acid. Every patient was randomized to receive 3 ml to 5 ml of the violet oil massage or dry massage. On alternate days, the patients received six treatments of 5 ml of oil massaged into the hand for seven minutes. Unobtrusive hand massage was chosen as a convenient administration method because the massage was given during dialysis sessions to both males and females.

Each patient was given a physical exam, had all medical history recorded, and completed a Scale and Visual Analogue Scale (VAS) questionnaire. A score of zero indicated a lack of pruritus while a score of nine represented severe symptoms.

This study was the first of its kind to evaluate the effect of massage with or without violet flower oil. The results showed that massage with violet flower oil was more effective in the treatment of uremic pruritus than massage alone. In conclusion, this study showed that massage alone can reduce skin dryness score, severity, location, and frequency of pruritus with hemodialysis patients. It appears that violet oil massage can further heighten the effect in lowering the dryness score because of the sedative, antipruritic, anti-inflammatory, and anti-hypertensive action in hemodialysis patients. This non-toxic, simple traditional remedy needs to be evaluated further by additional clinical studies. [22]

Viola odorata shows preliminary promise in treating difficulty urinating associated with an enlarged prostate. While short, a 2017 two-week, double-blind, placebo-controlled trial of a traditional Persian remedy blend of an infusion of violet *V. odorata* flowers, borage (*Echium amoenum*), and Chinese lantern (*Physalis alkekengi*), evaluated how effective it was for treating symptomatic benign prostate hyperplasia (BPH) in men. Prostate problems are common in the aging male population. At least 70% of 60-year-olds and 90% of men over 70 have benign prostatic hyperplasia. There are many theories as to why, but stromal and glandular cells of the prostate can become hyperproliferative (a high rate of growth) and result in a host of lower urinary tract symptoms.

There are many drug treatments and surgical procedures for the treatment of BPH but there is as strong desire for a natural, effective, and low side-effect treatment. A total of 86 male patients with symptoms of BPH were chosen in this randomized, double blind, 2-week placebo controlled single center trial.[23] The inclusion criteria focused on male patients with confirmed BPH, aged between 40 and 75, with a prostate volume more than 30, and an International Prostate Symptom Score of more than 13. The exclusion criteria included patients with diabetes, hypertension, cardiovascular disorders, hyperlipidemia, history of cardiac apoplexy, cerebral apoplexy, ischemic attack, and treatment with anti-BPH drugs within a month of the beginning the trial. The plants were all collected in different habitats ranging from a farm to the wild forests of Northern Iran. The plant materials were air dried in the shade and 50 g of each were ground and extracted with 80% ethanol, and then macerated for 48 hours. The solvent was removed by rotary evaporator and the extracts were mixed into a hydro-alcoholic solution with a final concentration of 1.5%, 1% and 1.5% for the *P. alkekengi*, *E. amoenum,* and *V. odorata* respectively.

Patients were assigned to receive 1 ml of the extract twice a day for two weeks. Baseline exams and exams after two weeks were performed for safety and to assess efficacy of treatment. The following were monitored during the treatment period:

- The value of hemoglobin, hematocrit, platelets, neutrophils, lymphocytes, and basophiles in blood
- Levels of serum electrolytes, fasting blood sugar, creatinine, BUN, elements, and liver enzyme
- Records of physical activities
- Serum examinations for measuring prostate specific antigen (PSA)

The International Prostate Symptom Score (IPSS) was utilized for evaluating the validity of patient's symptoms and responses to therapeutic protocol and further comparing the results among control and case groups.

The results demonstrated that all the men in treatment experienced significant decreases in symptoms of urinary excretion abnormalities including nocturia, incomplete urination, frequency, intermittency, urgency, and weak flow, plus prostate volume and excessive urine volume. The one exception was the symptom of urinary urgency, which did not change. IPSS scores significantly decreased in the treatment group compared to the placebo group. The prostate volume was considerably reduced in the treatment group. There were no significant changes in blood parameters between the two groups. The quality-of-life scores increased in the treatment group. In conclusion, the traditional Persian herbal medicine formula of the herbs *P. alkekengi, E. amoenum,* and *V. odorata* showed significant improvement in male patients with BPH. The combination indicated improvement in many of the expected lower urinary tract symptoms. Future research should examine each herb in the formula to investigate further action.[24]

The sedative and anti-inflammatory actions of *V. odorata* also may be effective for allergic rhinitis or hay fever. A 2020 study showed that *V. odorata* flower oil had significant positive effects on the symptoms of adults with allergic rhinitis.[25] The researchers enrolled 81 patients in this double-blind, randomized, placebo-controlled clinical trial. Patients were aged 18 to 60 with a diagnosis of mild to moderate allergic rhinitis, and with no impairment to daily activities. The exclusion criteria were pregnancy, lactation, concomitant respiratory illness, concomitant use of herbal medicine or steroid medications, and a history of allergy to violets. The fresh *V. odorata* flowers (200 g) were extracted in 1 liter of 70% ethanol and shaken for 5 days. The extract was dried under pressure to 40 g of material which was then dissolved in 4 liters of sweet almond oil. The oil was standardized to total phenolics at 28 mg/ml, expressed as gallic acid equivalence per ml of oil.

The participants were divided into two randomly assigned groups. One group received violet flower oil preparations every 12 hours, one drop per nostril. The placebo oil was used for the control group. Each group received treatment for two weeks. In this short period, the symptom scores between the groups reflected significant improvement by the violet oil group in reduction of symptoms of nose itching, sneezing, nasal congestion, rhinorrhea, eye itching, eye burning, eye tearing, sleep quality, daily activity, and fatigue compared to the placebo group. The effects of the violet oil preparations increased over time, becoming more effective and stronger from day 7 to day 14. All these improvements were significant.

In conclusion, *V. odorata* flower oil preparation was well accepted with no significant adverse events reported in the violet group compared to placebo. The findings demonstrate that *V. odorata* has potential as a natural, effective, and safe treatment of allergic rhinitis.[26] There is a need for longer studies to explore additional benefits from *V. odorata* flower oil.

Historical texts reveal that *V. odorata* flowers have the potential for improving sleep quality and for providing support for insomnia. Culpepper said, "[I]t likewise easeth pains in the head caused through want to sleep"[27] and this is supported by a 2017 critical review that concludes that the administration of *V. odorata* flower oil to patients with insomnia in a form of nasal drops for a one month period resulted in improvement of sleep and insomnia scores. [28] The *V. odorata* flower oil mentioned in the 2017 review is the infused oil.

As mentioned, the research review of traditional Persian medicine texts and research papers identified that *V. odorata* extracts were considered a traditional, herbal anti-metastatic treatment. Coupling this background with the presence of the constituent cycloviolacin-O2 found in *V. odorata* reveals the potential cytotoxic activity (toxic effects on cells). Cycloviolacin-O2 is thought to participate in the defense mechanism of *V. odorata* and has shown strong cytotoxic activity against a variety of drug-resistant and drug-sensitive human tumor cell lines, specifically primary chronic lymphocytic leukemia and ovarian carcinoma cells.[29] In a 2020 study,[30] researchers attempted to detect and compare the effects of *V. odorata* extract on malignant breast cancer cell lines (specific types of breast cancer cells) and breast cancer stem cells (cells from which all other specialized cells are created, such as for organs). The research was carried out on two frequently studied human breast cancer cell lines. Then, researchers performed an analysis and comparison on

Viola odorata, Mattiolo De materia medica (1564-1584).
Public Domain, plantillustrations.org

breast cancer stem cells treated with an alcoholic extraction of *V. odorata* on apoptosis and malignant characters of the breast cancer cell lines.

The results revealed that the extract of *V. odorata* induced cell death in the human breast cancer cell lines and their derived breast cancer stem cells through cell apoptosis. The *V. odorata* extract also demonstrated anti-migratory, anti-invasion, and anti-colony formation activity in the two human breast cancer cell lines. The research demonstrated a reduction of both the size and volume of tumors generated by the two breast cancer cell lines in a chicken embryo model. This study shows that the nontoxic extract of the traditional anticancer herb *V. odorata* has significant anticancer activity of human breast cancer cell lines. The data also suggested that the *V. odorata* extract targets mostly cancerous cells, not normal cells, and acts in a cell dependent manner. The study suggests future studies on *V. odorata* extract to treat breast cancer and other cancers as well.

A Final Word About *V. odorata*

In summary, *V. odorata* contains numerous therapeutic compounds that can be useful for various health conditions including digestive, cardiovascular, respiratory, skin, and oncology conditions and diseases. There are multiple clinical research studies to date, and a few of these are on humans. *V. odorata* has a long history as a traditional remedy and demonstrates a promising future that will be supported by well-designed clinical studies. Couple this with the fact that there are no reported food, drug, or supplement interactions associated with *V. odorata*, it is a valuable herb to grow in any home apothecary garden.

When *V. odorata* is in season, herbalists can prepare some simple violet remedies to enhance the home apothecary medicine chest. There is nothing more satisfying than gathering a basket of fresh violet flowers or leaves and preparing your own infused oil. Violet flowers are best gathered in the early morning on a warm summer day.

The following recipes provide amounts for the use of dried herbs. If you are using fresh herbs, double the quantity and leave them to wilt for six hours to reduce the water content. High water content will spoil the final product.

Violet Flower and Marshmallow Root Cough Syrup

1 ounce violet (*V. odorata*) flowers
1/2 ounce marshmallow (*Althaea officinalis*) root
1 1/2 pints distilled or filtered water
1 cup raw sugar
Honey, in the amount of the violet and marshmallow infusion
Glycerin, optional, 4 tablespoons for every 8 tablespoons of syrup

Prepare an infusion of the violet flowers and marshmallow root in the water. Let the mixture steep for 30 minutes, then strain and measure. For each cup of infusion, use one cup of honey.

Combine the sugar, honey, and lemon juice, and simmer over a low heat until it thickens and forms a syrup. Add the strained violet and marshmallow infusion. Return to heat if necessary to increase thickness. The optional vegetable glycerin can be added to help preserve the syrup for up to one week. Bottle and store in the refrigerator.

Infused Violet Flower and/or Violet Leaf Oil

The following three methods can be used to prepare either the fresh or dried *V. odorata* flowers or leaves. Note when using fresh violet flowers make sure to strain your finished product carefully and let the infused oil sit for 24 hours and then decant the oil. You may notice a small amount of water settling on the bottom of the oil. Leaving this water in the oil can lead to contamination and molding.

Water Bath Method

1 cup sweet almond (*Prunus amygdalus* var. *dulcis*) oil
1/2 ounce dried herb, or 1 ounce fresh herb

Pour the oil over the herbs in a stainless steel bowl. Heat over a water bath (a saucepan one-quarter filled with water) or double boiler, which should be simmering. Make sure the bowl is not sitting on the bottom of the pot but is floating in the water. Keep the lid on the oil. Stir occasionally and simmer the oil and herb over the water bath for 30 minutes. Be sure the oil does not become too hot. It should not smoke or bubble. It can burn easily and will develop an acrid smell if it overheats, which is very difficult to disguise.

Strain the plant material from the oil through four layers of unbleached muslin or some other very fine non-metal strainer. Strain twice, if necessary, as it is important to get all herbs out of the oil to prevent the oil from becoming rancid or moldy. If the oil has not extracted enough aroma from the plant material it is not recommended to add fresh material and reheat. You can, instead at this stage, add the fresh herb and prepare again using the solar method, described next.

Solar Method

Use the same quantities of herbs and oil as for the water bath method. The quantity of herb can be increased to produce a higher aroma intensity oil. Put the herbs in a jar with a tight-fitting lid and pour the oil over them. Make sure the herbs are completely covered with oil. Add 1 tablespoon of apple cider vinegar or white wine vinegar to help break down the plant material. Leave the jar to sit in the sun all day and in a warm cupboard at night for two weeks. You can leave it there longer if you choose, but at a minimum, two weeks.

Strain through four layers of unbleached cotton cheesecloth or muslin and repeat, if necessary, as plants can become moldy in oil. This process can be repeated two to three times to give stronger oil. The final product should be strong enough to leave an aroma when massaged on the skin. Always test infused oils by rubbing them on the skin.

Crockpot Method

Use the same quantities of herbs and oil as for water bath method. Place the herbs and oil in a crockpot and leave on a low heat for two hours. Follow the previous directions for straining.

How to Preserve Infused Oils

This is only necessary when you prepare large quantities that you intend to store for a while. Add the following preservatives once you have completed the infusion process and strained the oil thoroughly. Add 500 IU of natural mixed tocopherols or Vitamin E to 1 cup of infused oil. The shelf life of infused oils increases if the equipment and the bottles are clean and sterile. Prepare your infused oils using the same hygienic precautions as if you were canning food.

References

[1] Thulesius, O. *Nicholas Culpeper: English Physician and Astrologer.* Macmillan Press, 2001.

[2] *Viola odorata* L. GRIN-Global. Npgsweb.ars-grin.gov. (2021). Retrieved 3 June 2021, from https://npgsweb.ars-grin.gov/gringlobal/taxon/taxonomydetail?id=41733.

[3] *Viola tricolor L. subsp. curtisii (E. Forst.) Syme GRIN-Global.* Npgsweb. ars-grin.gov. (2021). Retrieved 3 June 2021, from https://npgsweb.ars-grin.gov/gringlobal/taxon/taxonomydetail?id=430392.

[4] *Greek Medicine - Asclepius.* Nlm.nih.gov. (2021). Retrieved 26 May 2021, from https://www.nlm.nih.gov/hmd/greek/greek_asclepius.html.

[5] Ibn Sina *[Avicenna] (Stanford Encyclopedia of Philosophy).* Plato. stanford.edu. (2021). Retrieved 26 May 2021, from https://plato.stanford.edu/entries/ibn-sina/.

[6] Qasemzadeh, M., Sharifi, H., Hamedanian, M., Gharehbeglou, M., Heydari, M., & Sardari, M. et al. (2015). "The Effect of Viola odorata Flower Syrup on the Cough of Children with Asthma." *Journal Of Evidence-Based Complementary & Alternative Medicine*, 20(4), 287-291. https://doi.org/10.1177/2156587215584862.

[7] Feyzabadi Z, Ghorbani F, Vazani Y, Zarshenas M. "A Critical Review on Phytochemistry, Pharmacology of *Viola odorata* L. and Related Multipotential Products in Traditional Persian Medicine." *Phytother.* Res. (2017) DOI:10.1002/ptr.5909.

[8] Svangard E, Burman R, Gunasekera S, Lo¨ vborg H, Gullbo J, Go¨ransson U. "Mechanism of action of cytotoxic cyclotides: cyclo-violacin O2 disrupts lipid membranes." *J Nat Prod.* 2007;70:643-647.

[9] Karioti A, Furlan C, Vincieri FF, Bilia AR. "Analysis of the constituents and quality control of Viola odorata aqueous preparations by HPLC-DAD and HPLC-ESI-MS." *Anal Bioanal Chem.* 2011;399:1715-1723.

[10] Pränting, M., Lööv, C., Burman, R., Göransson, U., & Andersson, D. I. (2010). "The cyclotide cycloviolacin O2 from Viola odorata has potent bactericidal activity against Gram-negative bacteria." *The Journal of Antimicrobial Chemotherapy*, 65(9), 1964–1971. https://doi.org/10.1093/jac/dkq220.

[11] Hellinger, R., Koehbach, J., Fedchuk, H., Sauer, B., Huber, R., Gruber, C. W., & Gründemann, C. (2014). "Immunosuppressive activity of an aqueous Viola tricolor herbal extract." *Journal of Ethnopharmacology*, 151(1), 299–306. https://doi.org/10.1016/j.jep.2013.10.044.

[12] Feyzabadi Z, Ghorbani F, Vazani Y, Zarshenas M. "A Critical Review on Phytochemistry, Pharmacology of *Viola odorata* L. and Related Multipotential Products in Traditional Persian Medicine." *Phytother. Res.* (2017) DOI:10.1002/ptr.5909.

[14] Christiano, D. (2018). "Swollen Anus: Causes, Symptoms, and Treatment." *Healthline*. Retrieved 2 June 2021, from https://www.healthline.com/health/swollen-anus.

[15] Feyzabadi Z, Ghorbani F, Vazani Y, Zarshenas M. "A Critical Review on Phytochemistry, Pharmacology of *Viola odorata* L. and Related Multipotential Products in Traditional Persian Medicine." *Phytother. Res.* (2017) DOI:10.1002/ptr.5909.

[16] To convert to common (kitchen) measures, 12 grams equals 2.4 teaspoons and 100 cc equals 3.38 ounces.

[17] Qasemzadeh, M., Sharifi, H., Hamedanian, M., Gharehbeglou, M., Heydari, M., & Sardari, M. et al. (2015). "The Effect of Viola odorata Flower Syrup on the Cough of Children With Asthma." *Journal Of Evidence-Based Complementary & Alternative Medicine*, 20(4), 287-291. https://doi.org/10.1177/2156587215584862.

[18] Culpeper, N. *The British herbal and family physician, for the cure of diseases incident to the human frame.* W. Nicholson and Sons, 1992.

[19] Hiroshige, K., Kabashima, N., Takasugi, M., & Kuroiwa, A. (1995). "Optimal dialysis improves uremic pruritus." *American Journal Of Kidney Diseases*, 25(3), 413-419. https://doi.org/10.1016/0272-6386(95)90102-7.

[20] Mettang, T., & Kremer, A. (2015). "Uremic pruritus." *Kidney International*, 87(4), 685-691. https://doi.org/10.1038/ki.2013.454.

[21] Khorsand A, Salari R, Noras M, Saki A, Jamali J, Sharifipour F, Mirmoosavi S, Ghazanfari S. "The effect of massage and topical violet oil on the severity of pruritus and dry skin in hemodialysis patients: A randomized controlled trial." *Complement Ther Med.* (2019) 45:248-253. DOI.org/10.1016/j.ctim.2019.06.015.

[22] Ibid

[23] Beiraghdar, F., Einollahi, B., Ghadyani, A., Panahi, Y., Hadjiakhoondi, A., & Vazirian, M. et al. (2017). "A two-week, double-blind, placebo-controlled trial of *Viola odorata, Echium amoenum and Physalis alkekengi* mixture in symptomatic benign prostate hyperplasia (BPH) men." *Pharmaceutical Biology*, 55(1), 1800-1805. https://doi.org/10.1080/13880209.2017.1328445.

[24] Ibid

[25] Yazdi N, Kardooni M, Namjuyan F, Vardanjani H, Tafazoli V, Jaladat A. "Efficacy of Sweet Violet (Viola odorata) flower oil on the symptoms of adults with allergic rhinitis: A double-blinded randomized placebo controlled clinical trial." *Complement Ther Med.* (2020)Vol. 51, 102408. doi.org/10.1016/j.ctim.2020.102408.

[26] Ibid

[27] Culpeper, N. *The British herbal and family physician, for the cure of diseases incident to the human frame.* W. Nicholson and Sons, 1922.

[28] Feyzabadi, Z., Ghorbani, F., Vazani, Y., & Zarshenas, M. (2017). "A Critical Review on Phytochemistry, Pharmacology of Viola odorata L. and Related Multipotential Products in Traditional Persian Medicine." *Phytotherapy Research*, 31(11), 1669-1675. https://doi.org/10.1002/ptr.5909./

[29] "Cycloviolacin-O2 - *Viola odorata (Sweet violet)*." Uniprot.org. (2021). Retrieved 27 May 2021, from https://www.uniprot.org/uniprot/P58434.

[30] Yousefnia, S., Naseri, D., Seyed Forootan, F., Tabatabaeian, M., Moattar, F., & Ghafghazi, T. et al. (2020). "Suppressive role of Viola odorata extract on malignant characters of mammosphere-derived breast cancer stem cells." *Clinical And Translational Oncology*, 22(9), 1619-1634. https://doi.org/10.1007/s12094-020-02307-9.

Dorene Petersen BA, DIP.NT, DIP.ACU, RH (AHG) is a New Zealand-trained Naturopath and aromatherapy, herbalism, and holistic wellness expert with decades of experience. She founded the American College of Healthcare Sciences (ACHS) in 1978 and has been President of the College since that time. Contact Dorene at dorenepetersen@achs.edu.

Glen Nagel ND, RH (AHG) is a practicing herbalist, licensed Naturopathic physician, and all-around herbal wise guy. He has a lifelong interest in plants and nature and believes in teaching with humor and hands-on experience. Glen is the Herbal Medicine Program Chair at ACHS.edu.

Pat Kenny

The Skinny on Violets:
Two Approaches to
Violets in Skin Care

Marge Powell

Violets have an exceptionally long history in the herbal apothecary related to skin conditions. Violets have earned a reputation of aiding oily, dry, and/or sensitive skin. Current research attributes this to the salicylic acid contained in the leaves and other parts of fresh violets. Salicylic acid disinfects and can dissolve tissue, which points to topical remedies to soften hard skin and treat corns and warts. Salicylic acid is also a known acne fighter. Sometimes people turn to willow bark as a source of salicylic acid, but willow bark contains salicin, which when taken orally is converted to salicylic acid by our digestive system. If used topically, our skin does not possess the enzymes to convert salicin to salicylic acid. Violet leaf is a rich source of salicylic acid and requires no conversion from salicin. In addition to the salicylic acid violet leaf contains vitamin C (an antioxidant and anti-inflammatory nutrient that improves skin tone and texture) and vitamin A (a widely accepted skin nutrient). When collected in spring violets contain twice as much vitamin C as the same weight of orange and more than twice the amount of vitamin A, gram for gram, when compared with spinach. Violet leaf is also fungicidal.

While violets could rest on their laurels as a soothing skin aid for eczema, rashes, hives, and other irritated skin conditions, they have a much more serious side. Violets have an active role in breast health, especially fibrocystic lumps, mastitis, plugged milk ducts, and as a natural adjunct in the treatment of breast cancer. In the 12th century Hildegard of Bingen used a violet salve to treat breast issues, including cancer. She heated the pressed juice of fresh violets with goat fat and olive oil to make an ointment for cysts, lumps, precancerous growths, sore muscles, and headaches. Avicenna, in the 10th century used *Viola odorata* to treat and calm cancer tumors.

Currently this historic approach to breast health is receiving support from modern research, much of it coming from Iran. One study has found that *Viola*

Violet bouquets keep blooms fresh until they can be processed.
Susan Belsinger

odorata can be toxic to certain breast cancer cells and provides antioxidant activity in the metastasis of breast cancer. They found that an alcohol/water extract of *Viola odorata* significantly inhibited the cell proliferation. Another study has found that an extract of *Viola odorata* prevented oral cancer growth in rats but that the effectiveness of the treatment was dependent on dosage of the extract. The higher the dosage, the greater the prevention.

Viola odorata occurs naturally in much of Europe as well as in Iran, but not in the United States. Our most common native violet is *Viola sororia* which differs from *Viola odorata* in its lack of significant fragrance. Fortunately, when it comes to medicinal properties, violets are interchangeable.

The question arises as to how to best make use of these beneficial violet properties topically. At this point, I would like to interject two strong caveats: Some people are sensitive to the external application of violets which can result in itching and burning. Always check for this sensitivity before proceeding to use any topical violet formulations.

The information offered in this article is in no way meant to act as a substitute for professional medical advice or professional medical treatment. Rather it is offered in the spirit of broadening the knowledge of what is available in our natural world.

I propose taking a dual approach to the topical application of violets, an ointment and a cream. Both use violet-infused oil as their foundation. Infused oil is a simple concoction. In its most basic form, it is simply plant material that sits in oil over a period of time with the intent to extract the beneficial contents of the plant cells into the oil. However, there are several things to consider.

> Should fresh or dried botanic material be used?
> Which oils to use?
> What is the ratio of botanic material to oil?
> How long should the mixture infuse?

I usually favor dried plant material for oil infusion because fresh material almost always molds before the infusion has adequately infused. Appendix A is a list of various oils that can be used and their topical medicinal behaviors. The ratio of botanic material is flexible and will vary considerably according to the use of fresh or dry botanic material and the nature of the botanic material. I have a minimum infusion period of six weeks for my oils but infusing beyond six weeks causes no harm if there is no mold or deterioration

Fresh violets gathered for the oil infusion. *Marge Powell*

of the plant material.

For the violet-infused oils for these formulas, I gathered 1.6 ounces of fresh violet leaf and flowers and dried them for a week. The dried violets weighed .4 ounces. I infused the dried violets in a mixture of 6 ounces of sweet almond oil and 6 ounces of organic extra virgin olive oil. I chose the oils for their healing, nourishing, and anti-inflammatory attributes. If you calculate the plant-to-oil ratio of the fresh material, it is 1.6:12 or 7.5 times the amount of fresh plant material for the oil. If you calculate the plant-to-oil ratio of the dried material, it is .4:12 or 30 times the amount of fresh plant material for the oil. The oil infused 9 weeks prior to constructing the formulas. I strained the oil into a jar which resulted in 10.7 ounces of infused oil. No matter how much I squeeze the plant material dry when straining, there is always a loss of oil from the original measure of the oil.

This oil is medicinal and can be used as is to massage directly onto dry, irritated skin or used as an ingredient in formulae for salves, lotions, creams, lip balms, or soaps. Poultice-like applications of a cloth saturated with this infused oil is a classic recipe for dissolving lumps and cysts. Violet absolute can be added to the infused oil, and it can be massaged into breasts to maintain breast health and as adjunct support for breast cancer and cysts.

Infused oil prior to straining. *Marge Powell*

However, this can be a messy process which results in spilled oil and stained clothes. The solution is to use the infused oil as a basis for an ointment, a cream, or a lotion. The difference between these products is their water content. An ointment contains no water, a cream contains about 50% water (if this water is a hydrosol, it can add additional benefits to the cream), and a lotion contains less than 50% water, sometimes much less. There are hairsplitting definitions of the differences between an ointment, salve, or a balm, but for the purposes of this article I will consider them synonymous.

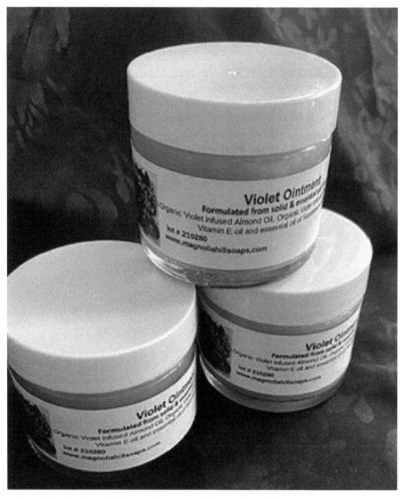

Finished and labeled violet ointment. *Marge Powell*

Violet Ointment

You will need

5.1 ounces of the above violet-infused oil
.8-ounce natural beeswax (this should be brown, not white)
10 drops violet absolute*
.2 ounce sandalwood essential oil*
.2 ounce vitamin E oil (as a preservative)
Glass jars with covers
A saucepan
Thermometer
Funnel
Labels
Alcohol
A large towel

*Sandalwood essential oil and violet absolute are rather expensive. I chose them because they are helpful to oily, dry, or sensitive skin. Less expensive substitutes could be lavender, geranium, or patchouli essential oils. You can combine essential oils if you choose. However, I would limit the combination to three different oils. The important thing is to use essential oils and not fragrance oils. If all you have available are fragrance oils, it is best to not use any scented oil.

The Process:
Lay out the towel on a table. This will be your workspace and it is easier to wash a towel that has oil dripped on it than to clean it from a table.

Spray or wipe your jars and lids with the alcohol.

Place the infused oil, the vitamin E oil, and the beeswax in the saucepan and heat to about 165°F.

Cool to about 150°F.

Remove the saucepan from the heat and stir in the essential oils and the violet absolute if you are using it.

Pour the oil mixture into the jars and cover.

When cool, label with the name of the ointment, the ingredients, and the date.

This ointment can also be used for skin, abrasions, insect bites, eczema, varicose veins, hemorrhoids, and to heal wounds. David Hoffman suggests that it has a role in a long-term approach to rheumatism.

The cream formula will have a water phase and an oil phase, and this will be emulsified. The water phase will incorporate both violet extract and violet hydrosol. The violet extract was made by combining .5 ounces of fresh violet leaf with 2 ounces of 100 proof vodka. This mixture was whirred in a mini food processor to expose as much of the leaf as possible to the vodka. This should be aged about 3 weeks. I made the hydrosol by distilling 1.1 ounces of fresh violet leaf with 16 ounces of water using a process that I describe in the IHA conference proceedings of 2009. This yielded 14.9 ounces of hydrosol. Violet hydrosol can be purchased on the internet or distilled water can be used in its stead. Violet extract was used in the Iranian study that concluded there was an effect on tumor growth. Violet hydrosol is reputed to sooth irritated and inflamed skin.

Violet flowers to be dried for violet-infused oil. *Susan Belsinger*

Violet Cream

You will need

5.6 ounces of the above violet-infused oil
.5 ounce natural beeswax (this should be brown, not white)
3 ounces violet hydrosol
.5 ounce violet extract
.1 ounce ylang ylang essential oil
.1 ounce geranium essential oil
.3 ounce vitamin E oil (as a preservative)
Glass jars with covers
A saucepan
Thermometer
Funnel
Labels
Alcohol
A large towel
Stick or immersion blender
Small, deep bowl

The Process:

1. Lay out the towel on a table. This will be your workspace and it is easier to wash a towel that has oil dripped on it than to clean it from a table.
2. Spray or wipe your jars and lids with the alcohol.
3. Place the infused oil, the vitamin E oil, and the beeswax in the saucepan and heat to about 165°F.
4. Cool to about 150°F.
5. Meanwhile, add the hydrosol, extract, and essential oils to the small deep bowl. Whirr once or twice with the immersion blender.
6. Slowly add the hot oil mixture to the hydrosol mixture, continually blending with the immersion blender. The mixture will look like globs but keep blending and it will even itself out.
7. Pour the mixture into the jars and cover.
8. When cool, label with the name of the ointment, the ingredients, and the date.

Both the cream and the ointment can be used to provide the herbal benefits of violet. Traditionally, these benefits are claimed to be pain relief, lymph support, edema reduction, lump and cyst management, and anti-inflammatory support, and, due to the salicylic acid, nourishment of the nerves and healing wounds and bruises. Some herbalists use violet as an adjunct in dealing with grief and loss.

Toward the end of the stick blending. *Marge Powell*

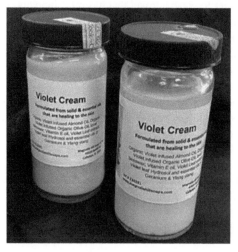

Cream bottled and labeled. *Marge Powell*

Appendix A
The Oils and their attributes

Oil	Attribute
Almond Oil	Softens, smooths, conditions skin, rich in protein, emollient, nourishing. The phytosterols are anti-inflammatory and help relieve itching from eczema. The vitamin E acts as an antioxidant. Slow to go rancid.
Apricot Kernel and Peach Kernel oil	Have the same properties as almond oil but are more expensive. Use in combination with other oils.
Avocado oil	Therapeutic, healing; contains protein, amino acids and large amounts of vitamins A, B, D, and E, and the glycerides of many fatty acids. The vitamin B helps with damaged skin and cell regeneration. It is easily absorbed by the skin; regenerates skin cells and softens tissues. It is the most nourishing oil (along with wheat germ oil) and the most penetrating (along with hazelnut oil). It will become sticky if used in large quantities and on a large area. Use in combination with other oils. Do not allow the oil to chill or it will precipitate.
Cranberry seed oil or Raspberry seed oil	Very expensive, contains essential fatty acids (EFA), can protect against sunburn. Use in combination with other oils.
Cocoa butter	Conditioning, skin softener, lays down protective layer that holds moisture to the skin. Use in combination with other oils.
Coconut oil	Polyphenols provide anti-oxidizing, anti-inflammatory, and anti-itching properties. Can be considered anti-bacterial. Moisturizing, cleansing, can be drying in large quantities. Use in combination with other oils.
Borage Seed oil or Black Currant oil	Contains GLA (gamma linoleic acid). Use in combination with other oils.
Evening Primrose oil	Expensive, contains GLA which is useful for scaly dry skin and dandruff. Use in combination with other oils.

Appendix A
The Oils and their attributes

Oil	Attribute
Grapeseed Oil	Polyphenols provide anti-oxidizing, anti-inflammatory, and anti-itching properties. Clear and odorless, has no allergic effects on the skin; gives a satin smooth finish but is not greasy. Inexpensive. Shelf life can be extended with a 5% addition of wheat germ oil. Use in combination with other oils.
Hazelnut oil	Along with avocado is the most penetrating – penetrates easily and deeply. Stimulates circulation and nourishes the skin. Good for massage. Contains tannins that will make the oil feel drier than other oils. Polyphenols provide anti-oxidizing, anti-inflammatory, and anti-itching properties.
Hemp seed oil	Hemp seed oil softens, soothes, and promotes flexibility by working between surface cells, helping to lubricate, reduce flaking, and revive the skin's intercellular lipids. The oil contains 50% to 60% linoleic acid and is the only high EFA oil that also contains GLA. The GLA increases skin barrier repair and is moisturizing. Because its EFA profile so closely resembles the skin's natural lipids, hemp seed oil instantly counteracts the effects of degreasing and dehydration, conditions that produce dry skin. It can quickly moisturize and condition. Use in combination with other oils.
Jojoba oil	Is really a wax. It is indigestible to bacteria (and humans). It is good for acne because it dissolves sebum and makes the skin feel satin smooth. It contains tannins that create antioxidant and astringent properties. Softens skin by penetrating it. Contains a fatty alcohol (octacosanol) that can soothe very dry skin.
Olive oil	Is a calming emollient, nourishing, healing, and a good moisturizer because it attracts external moisture and holds the moisture close to the skin and forms a breathable film to prevent internal moisture loss. It is good for arthritis and relieves the itching of skin ailments. If you use cold pressed first pressing, the scent can overpower other scents. Contains sitosterol which provides an ant-inflammatory effect and is very good for dry skin.

Appendix A
The Oils and their attributes

Oil	Attribute
Rosehip seed oil (Mosqueta)	It is unique among vegetable oils in containing retinol (Vitamin A). Rose hip seed oil is high in the essential fatty acids—linoleic acid or omega-3, and linolenic acid or omega-6. It is helpful for a variety of skin conditions, including dermatitis, acne and eczema, for mature and sun-burnt skin as well as brittle nails. Use in combination with other oils.
Sesame oil	Rich in vitamins A and E. Its scent might be objectionable. In Scandinavia it is used for dry eczema and psoriasis. It washes easily out of clothes. It is remarkably high in phytosterols which provide anti-inflammatory and ant-itching properties.
Shortening	Will have the same benefits as the oils from which it was hydrogenated - sometimes called vegetable tallow. NOT RECOMMENDED.
Sunflower oil	Has a very short shelf life – must have an antioxidant to act as a preservative. But it has vitamin E which is useful for some skin conditions. Use in combination with other oils.
Wheat germ oil	A natural antioxidant, vitamin rich – it has high levels of vitamin E plus carotene and vegetable lecithin which nourishes skin cells and hinders moisture loss. The carotenoids provide photo protective properties and soothe UVB damaged skin. Contains phytosterols which provide anti-inflammatory and ant-itching properties and skin barrier repair. It is especially good for dry skin, helps healing, and reduces scarring from wounds and acne. It is expensive and sticky so use in combination with other oils. (It can be added at a rate of 5% to other oils to extend their shelf life).

References

Bennett, Robin Rose. *The Gift of Healing Herbs*. North Atlantic Books, 2014.

Blankenspoor, Juliet. "Violets Edible and Medicinal Uses." 4/13/2016. Chestnut School of Herbal Medicine. chestnutherbs.com/violets-edible-and-medicinal-uses/. Accessed 5/18/21.

Erichsen-Brown, Charlotte. "Medicinal and other uses of North American plants." (Reprint of original 1979 issue.) Dover Publications Inc., NY 1989.

Sanaz Helli, Hossein Damghani, Daryoush Mohajeri, Mehran Mesgari AbbasiRana Attaran, and Maryam Zahed, "Evaluation of the Effect of Two Different Systemic Doses of Viola Odorata on Prevention of Induced Tongue Dysplasia in Rats." *Journal of Dentistry Shiraz University of Medical Sciences* 2016 Sep; 17(3): 185–192. Accessed from US National Library of Medicine, National Institutes of Health, 5/17/21.

Hoffman, David. *The New Holistic Herbal*. Barnes and Noble, 1990.

Hiva Alipanah, Mohammad Reza Bigdeli, and Mohammad Ali Esmaeili. "Inhibitory Effect of *Viola odorata* Extract on Tumor Growth and Metastasis in 4T1 Breast Cancer Model." *Iranian Journal of Pharmaceutical Research*. Winter 2018;17(1): 276-291. Accessed from Pubmed.gov 5/17/21.

Powell, Marge. "The Shortcut to Herbal Distillates." *International Herb Association Proceedings of Annual Members Meeting and Conference.* July 18, 2009. 8-11.

Smith, Erin, "Plant Profile: Violet." *Integrative Family Medicine of Asheville.* www.integrativeasheville.org/plant-profile-violet/. Accessed 5/18/21.

"The Virtues of Violets – The Health Benefits of Violets." 4/29/2014. *The Herbal Academy*. theherbalacademy.com/health-benefits-of-violets/. Accessed 5/17/21.

Weed, Susun S. *Healing Wise*. Ash Tree Publishing, 1989.

----- *Breast Cancer? Breast Health*. Ash Tree Publishing, 1996.

Marge Powell has been an herbalist for over 30 years and an avid plant person her entire life.

Her herbal interests span both the culinary, the medicinal and body care as well as growing herbs. She completed a medicinal herbal apprenticeship with Susun Weed and was introduced to herbal body care in workshops conducted by Rosemary Gladstar.

Marge is a passionate cook and most of her cooking is herb-enhanced. She teaches classes in cooking with herbs, making your own medicines, creating lotions and ointments, making soap, and blending scents. She has conducted hands-on workshops on these and a variety of other herbal topics across the United States. She has also lectured in Lifelong Learning workshops in NE Florida. In 2000 she incorporated Magnolia Hill Soap Co., Inc. (www. magnoliahillsoaps.com) and in 2011 she added Magnolia Hill Nursery, which wholesales organic herbs and heirloom vegetables to local garden centers.

She is currently a board member of the International Herb Association (IHA) and the International Herb Association Foundation and is past president of IHA's former Southeastern Region. She has had numerous herbal articles published in IHA's annual Herb of the Year publications.

Detail, common blue violet bloom. *Susan Belsinger*

Wedding cake decorated with 400 candied violets. *Jane Stevens*

The Transformative Power of Violets

Jane Hawley Stevens

Violets spring forth, bringing the coolness of the recently thawed earth. As the leaves poke through the ground, this harbinger of spring gets me excited, filling up my lawn and garden with their heart-shaped leaves and amethyst blooms. Their presence tugs at my heart, bringing springtime memories of picking violets. I used to make a violet body oil that had dried violets in every bottle, so I would lovingly pick and store them for the year's use. Violets are fleeting and don't hold their color long. We had to carefully dry them and store them in tins in the freezer to hold the color. Drying and not freezing them did **not** hold this ephemeral color.

My wedding cake was decorated with 400 candied violets by my neighbor, Laura Lynch, who recently turned 101. She carefully collected the violets in her yard, dipped them in egg whites, then in sugar and allowed them to dry. These are stunning decorations for your springtime desserts.

This year's harvest was for violet syrup. Violet syrup has a rich tradition in Europe, where it has been used for centuries to assist healthy pulmonary function. The visual aspect of the captured violet color is divine and can uplift a glass of sparkling water or create a gorgeous martini.

The color violet is thought of as purple, but it is beyond purple in the color spectrum, between purple and ultraviolet. Violet has the shortest wavelength and the highest vibration in the visible spectrum of light. With that knowledge, endings and beginnings are implied. Violets carry that message of transformation, changing the earth from brown and grey to lush green and violet.

In esoteric terms, violet is the color of the Crown Chakra, connecting us to the Divine. Violets embrace my Buddha statue in the seventh section of my Chakra Garden (as well as my lawn and gardens because I can't bear to weed them away). The Chakra System is an Eastern way of understanding the body systems, connecting the physical, emotional and spiritual aspects of our human experience. Chakra means *wheel* in Sanskrit and refers to the spinning energy as it moves up through our body.

The heart-shaped leaves evoke sentiments connected to the soul. Just look at people's response to violets or feel your own. The color violet is cleansing and purifying. It is the color of magic and ritual, connecting mystery and mysticism.

On a more botanical note, much mystery in violets is hidden beneath the ground. Did you know that violets have a secondary reproductive system that creates seeds beneath the ground, never opening these petals to the light of day? Known as cleistogamous flowers (cleistogamy derives from the Greek words *cleistos,* meaning closed, and *gamos,* indicating marriage; thus cleistogamy translates to closed marriage), these are true flowers, but are white, never turning blue because they have no need to attract a pollinator. These underground flowers develop into fruits, then seeds, and release the seeds directly into the soil. No wonder gardens and yards fill up with these botanical beauties so freely!

Violets stir within us a sense of companionship, noted in the species of our state flower of Wisconsin, *Viola sororia,* from the Latin word *sororitas*, meaning "sisterhood, of or pertaining to sisters." I imagine the sorority of violet sisters in their delightful alliance, enjoying their metamorphosis into adulthood. In the old English Language of Flowers, the blue violet was used to speak the message of faithfulness, another sentiment evoking friendship. It is appropriate that the yellow violet, *Viola pubescens,* is found in our woods, carrying the message of "rural happiness" in the language of flowers.

A close relative, the wild pansy, *V. tricolor*, is named after the Greek word *panacea*, for reducing excessive and unwanted thoughts, or from *pan* meaning all and *akos*, meaning heal, translated as the universal remedy. This theory, different than the more common one of the French origin, works for me!

Violet's cooling and demulcent nature can be employed internally and topically. The softening nature is like a sister to calendula, *Calendula officinalis,* and has been used for centuries to soothe and comfort inflammation. Violet is well known as an aid for effective lymphatic response, used topically or internally. Violet has an affinity for breast tissue and is a traditional herb for breast massage. Like red clover, violets have a long history in the treatment of rapid cell division.

According to Euell Gibbons, the famous 1970's folk edible wild guru, "The violet is a fine, pleasing plant of Venus, of mild nature and in no way harmful." This gentle nature of violets makes them useful for all ages, with no recommended dose necessary. Just use the flowers and leaves for their nutrients and their virtues. In fact, the leaves can be added to soups and stews as a nutrient-dense thickener. **Note:** The roots should not be consumed; they could cause vomiting.

Although our native violets do not carry the seductive scent of the European violets, I had the great fortune to visit my daughter as a college student in Aix-en-Provence, France. It was late March as we entered a park in the evening. There it was—scented violets saturating the air! I was truly in heaven on earth. Violets have a way of transporting us to the otherworld, as they carry the energy to break boundaries through our everyday moments, into the sublime.

Violet Martini

Go to the resale shop and find the proper martini glasses, tiny and triangular. Fill with crushed ice. Pour a shot of gin or vodka in the glass. Add 1 to 2 tablespoons of Four Elements Violet Syrup and stir. Garnish with a slice of lemon or an organic canned cherry. Toast to your good fortune and feel gratitude for Nature's loveliness.

Violet Martini. *Jane Stevens*

References

Gibbons, Euell. *Stalking the Healthful Herbs*. David McKay Company Inc., 1966.

Hottes, Alfred. *Garden Facts and Fancies*. Mead & Company, 1949.

Joseph, Michael. *The Language of Flowers*. Penguin, 1968.

Stern, William. *Botanical Latin, New Edition*. David & Charles, 1983.

https://www.theoi.com/Ouranios/AsklepiasPanakeia.html. Accessed October 28, 2021.

https://wisconsinpollinators.com/Garden/G_Violets.aspx. Accessed October 28, 2021.

A pioneer of the organic farming movement and the natural products industry, **Jane Stevens** is an advocate for health on earth. Recently named Midwest Organic Farmer of the year (2020), her sustainable farming practices are the roots of her herbal wellness line, Four Elements Organic Herbals. When Jane is not busy writing, propagating herbs, or managing the business, you may find her foraging in the woods, reflecting in her Chakra Garden, or camping, biking, skiing, or skating with family and friends. Visit Jane's website at www.fourelementsherbals.com; contact her at info@fourelementsherbals.com.

Blue violets. *Susan Belsinger*

The Mothering Violaceae

Gail Wood Miller

When I had a cottage close to the ocean on Staten Island, I treasured my deep blue violets. They rose between the pieces of flagstone on my patio in the back, facing northwest. I suspect they were a variety of *Viola palmata* crossed with *V. sororia*. Tiny white chickweed flowers joined them. The violets opened in mid-April, in time for me to carefully cut stems, spread out the delicate skirt-petals on tissue, cover them, and weigh them down heavily with dictionaries for a week or so of pressing before I sent them, glued to a card, to my godmother, for Mother's Day. Ah! No wonder, then, violets are sometimes called Godmothers—or Godfathers. (Men can be motherly, after all.) So, I came to associate violets with Mother's Day before I learned how helpful they are in balancing hormones. When I heard they might help cancer patients, I was hooked. I see the *Viola* family as one, expansive mother.

After mid-April, the more reticent violets appeared in my shady southside garden and lawn, surrounded by their dark-green, heart-shaped circlets of leaves, often larger than the flowers. The leaves abounded, sneaking to the side of my cottage as well. It was Susun Weed who introduced me to eating violets. A nurse-midwife handed me Weed's book on menopause when I needed it; a lovely part of my "treatment," then, was making the leaves a regular salad addition. However, Weed cautions in *Healing Wise*, externally the leaves can cause topical distress, even "minor eruptions on sensitive skin" (240). I hadn`t had that experience, though. Perhaps it`s because of the wide range of qualities violets can have, depending on where they live. All, however, have the reputation of being not only edible, but also healthful, in the above-ground parts of the plant. Weed mentions reports of large quantities of violets credited with helping patients deal with cancer. No wonder she calls the violet an "ally."

J. T. Garrett tells of a Cherokee elder referring to violet as *ou ste*—the "little plant with a big punch" (245). Some members of the seed-producing *Viola* family can both self-mutate and join forces with another *viola* to form a hybrid. Pollination can come from wind, insects, or other animals, bringing the pollen from the male part of a plant to fertilize the female part of a plant: in the case of *Viola*, this can come from itself, or from another *Viola*. Fertilization of seed and spore depends on a suitable environment. For ferns, this is usually a moist, wet surface for the sperm cells to land on. Although used popularly in Cherokee medicine for chest ailments, the violet, on its own, is also used to treat inflammation, nervous disorders, and insomnia. When it mates with spore-producing American maidenhair fern (*Adiantum pedatum*), the smoke helps asthma and fever. When it mates with seed-producing dogwood (*Cornus*), it can be used—as it was in earlier Southeastern tribes—to alleviate bronchitis and assorted pains, including headache. Without pollination, the violet can send out runners and reproduce itself (for this reason, it is considered a weed in some areas). In botanical terms, this is referred to as the plant being androgenous, hermaphroditic, or—perfect.

Violets historically signified modesty and innocence. Josephine Bonaparte loved them. She held them in her hands and decorated her clothing with them at her wedding to Napoleon. He gave violets to her at every anniversary. (Napoleon, in fact, was called Corporal Violet by his friends; the violet became his secret symbol, worn, in flower or its color, by his followers.) They were, ultimately, on her grave—placed by her widower Napoleon, as violets were a tradition at funerals, though more so in ancient Rome and Greece.

Ah, "sweet violets, sweeter than the roses" the Joseph Emmet song goes. One of the reasons for this reputation is the delicate smell some people note. It varies, of course, in different types of violets. Perhaps my fondness for the violet, *Viola sororia* in particular, isn`t exclusively for its aesthetic simplicity, its warmth of blues and purples, and its glistening green leaves—but actually because the delicate smell quickly dissipates. Like many others with pollen sensitivity, the less the smell, the more content I am. Violet's maternal magic wand is *ionine*, temporarily short-circuiting our sense of smell. How motherly of her to do this.

The *Viola* cousin noted for its smell, its odor, is, appropriately, *Viola odorata*. It is commonly known as the Sweet Violet, or the English Garden Violet. Some people call her the Common Violet, but I think that`s an insult. This is the dramatic sister. She originally comes from Eurasia, but has been cultivated elsewhere. She flaunts her fragrance. Not only are tons of her flowers made into perfumes, but she tastes as beguiling as she smells, and finds her way into candies. She is also, being motherly, often a preferred source for the healing oil violet is known for. Zohre Feyzabadi has led researchers into key studies of

Viola odorata's health benefits, based on traditional Persian medicine. Violet oil—VO in the studies—was the source for improving sleep in patients with chronic insomnia, administered in pre-sleep nose drops for a month (66 mg VO). Before making VO (sounds charming, doesn`t it?), consult a reliable source for instructions in making it, as it can be quite strong; there may also be strength variants in the species of violet you`re using.

While *Viola odorata* is more frequently reported on as a healer for an extraordinary array of ailments, she is not alone in these capacities. All her violet sisters have, for example, antioxidant and anti-inflammatory qualities (even helping varicose veins) via the rutin in the leaves, which are also high in vitamins A and C. Violaceae mothers us beyond the familiar violets, violas, and pansies. Violet's cousins includes a group favored as emetics, including *Anchietea salutaris*, *Corynostylis hybanthus*, and *Hybanthus ipecacuanha*, all natives of South America. For more details on the plethora of ways members of the Violaceae family help with healing, see the National Institutes of Health`s online National Library of Medicine.

A branch of the extended, worldwide *Viola* family has its own sorority, appropriately called *sororia* (meaning "of a sister"). One of the sisters is an international beauty queen, the white *Viola sororia* 'Albiflora'. In 2002 the Royal Horticultural Society (RHS) crowned her abundant flowers with the Award of Garden Merit. An Eastern North American native, she represents, as state flower, in her blue species, the states of Rhode Island, New Jersey, Illinois, and Wisconsin, where she is nicknamed the Confederate Violet, as her pale greyish blue color is similar to Confederate uniforms during the Civil War.

Violet's sister, the pansy (*Viola xwittrockiana*) is often considered more fragile than the violet. She has a mischievous side, and is consequently called "Little Stepmother," or *Stiefmutterchen*, in German. One theory addresses the difference between the pansy's five petals from those of the violet. The violet's petals face up. The pansy petals are divided: four face up, and one down, making it similar to, but different from, the violet. Another theory is that the pansy petals represent a mother and daughters, as the petals are often more distinctive from each other than those of the violet.

Violaceae mother appreciates the diversity of her children, and has adapted them to climes all over the world. In this country alone, Ezra Brainerd in 1921 reported on identifying some 2,000 species. He chose to study the *Viola* because, as George P. Burns's introduction to Brainerd's text tells us, it grew "in the wild" and was a "well defined species with numerous intermediate forms—hybrids or elementary species" (1921, 14). Brainerd studied *Viola* for over 25 years, often with his daughter, Frances Viola. He was "painfully aware of the confusion that had arisen from the publication of scores of obscure and illegitimate species...based on scanty or immature material" (1905, 1). He was particularly interested in natural hybridization and mutation, through collecting seeds, planting, and observing.

His daughter, Frances Viola Brainerd Baird—omitting her first name as an author, wrote on wild violets, including some she initially discovered, such as two versions of the *Viola rafinesquei*. She continued the work of her father and furthered the research of Frederick Traugott Pursch, a German scientist who had collected specimens on the Lewis and Clark expedition. (There seems to be a debate in the herbal community on whether *Viola* are native or naturalized citizens. It seems to me the data on native species, dating back to the 1600s, outweighs the opposing argument. The National Institutes of Health`s medical library continues to report on further discoveries.)

Our *Viola* mother is also a romantic...Violets were a popular aphrodisiac. Water nymphs, the Nereids or Naiads, gathered violets growing wildly on banks of rivers and streams, making bouquets to welcome Ion, mythological founder of the Ionians, of Athens. (Hence, the chemical name of her magic, *ionone*.) Myths about Ion vary, but seem to agree that he was the illegitimate son of Apollo, his future saved by Delphic priestesses, including an eventual reunion with his mother, Creusa (who left newborn Ion in a cave to die). Some tales say Ion responded to Athenians' plea for help in their consequently successful war against the Eleusinians. Ion became king of Athens, and divided the land into quarters, each for one of his sons.

The Greek definition of *ion* as "to go" certainly fits the life Ion led. It also became a scientific term in 1834, naming an element—an ion—moving toward an oppositely-charged electron. Ion can also refer to the color purple (which some violets are). Purple is the traditional color of mourning in European-based cultures. But an adventurous form of "to go" leads to the water nymphs. They protected rivers and streams, guarding the area between the underworld and the human one. They welcomed the god Ion to Attica with bouquets of violets, growing on the banks of their territories. Venus may have been a Siren sister, leading to the nymphs' reputation as being connected to her, goddess of love, fertility, beauty, and prosperity. And, among the many magical, wonderful qualities that have come to define violet, one is *inspiring prosperity*.

This is a parent's wish—for her children to have prosperity. She helps them to help themselves. Foremost, she loves and accepts them unconditionally. Sara Ruddick evolved this concept to develop a new branch of philosophy, one that could, she purports, promote world peace—*maternal thinking*. Anyone, male or female, Ruddick says, can accept others unconditionally: we need to think like a mother. The *Viola* family already does.

References

Ackerman, Diane. *A Natural History of the Senses*. Random House, 1990.

Baird, Viola Brainerd. *Wild Violets of North America*. University of California Press, 1942.

-----. Viola Brainerd. "A Natural Violet Hybrid." In *Madrono: A West American Journal of Botany, Vol. 3*. California Botanical Society, 1936, pp 325-327. www.biodiversitylibrary.org/page/47919252#page/365/mode/1up. Accessed 25 May 2021.

Bennett, Robin Rose. *The Gift of Healing Herbs*. North Atlantic Books, 2014.

Blankespoor, Juliet. "Violet's Edible and Medicinal Uses." *Castanea*. Chestnut School of Herbal Medicine, 2016. www.chestnutherbs.com/violets-edible-and-medicinal-uses/. Accessed 26 Mar. 2021.

Brainerd, Ezra. "Notes on New England Violets, II." *Journal of the New England Botanical Club, Vol 7, No 73*, Jan. 1905. https://books.google.com/books. Accessed 25 May 2021.

-----. *Violets of North America* (George P. Burns, Intro.) University of Vermont Agricultural Experiment Station Bulletin 224, Burlington, VT: Free Press Printing Co., 1921. https://babel.hathitrust.org/cgi/pt?id=uiug.30112019892683&view=1up&seq=5. Accessed 25 May 2021.

Comenius University. *The Legend of Violet—the Flower*. Bratislava, Slovakia, www.comenius-legends.blogspot.com/2010/07/legend-of-violet.html. Accessed 27 Mar. 2021.

Corrington, Julian D. "Violets." In *BIOS, Vol. 25, No. 3*, 1954, pp 160-168.

Emmet, Joseph K.. "Sweet Violets" from *Fritz Among the Gypsies*, Church & Company, 1882.

Feyzabadi, Zohre; Ghorbani, Fariba; Vazani, Yasaman; Zarshenas, Mohammad M. "A Critical Review on Phytochemistry, Pharmacology of Viola odorata L. and Related Multipotential Products in Traditional Persian Medicine." *Phytotherapy Research*, 31 (11), Nov. 2017, pp 1669-1675.

Feyzabadi, Zohre; Jafari, F.; Kamali, S. H.; Ashayeri, H.; Badiee Aval, S.; Esfahani, M.M.; Sadeghpour, O.. "Efficacy of Viola odorata in Treatment of Chronic Insomnia." *Iran Red Crescent Medical Journal* 16 (12), Dec. 2014, p 17511.

Field Museum, The. "Viola odorata." *The Morton Arboretum.* Symbiota, SEINet, Arizona-New Mexico Chapter, www.swbiodiversity.org/seinet/taxa/index.php?taxon=Viola+odorata. Accessed 27 Mar. 2021.

Folger Library. "Beyond Home Remedy: Women, Medicine, and Science." www.Folgerpedia.folger.edu. Accessed 27 Mar. 2021.

Garrett, J. T. *The Cherokee Herbal: Native Plant Medicine from the Four Directions.* Bear & Company, 2003.

Harper, Douglas. "Ion." *Online Etymology Dictionary*, 2021. www.etymonline.com/word/ion. Accessed Sept. 13, 2021.

Homestratosphere. *37 Different Types of Violets for Your Garden.* www.homestratosphere.com/types-of-violets/. Accessed 28 Mar. 2021.

Jones, Diana L. "The Medicinal Properties and Health Benefits of Violets." *Good Witches Homestead*, 2017-2021, www.goodwitcheshomestead.com/. Accessed 3 Apr. 2021.

Little, R. John and McKinney, Landon E. "Violaceae." *Flora of North America.* 2020, www.beta.floranorthamerica.org/Violaceae. Accessed 28 Mar. 2021.

Lopez, Elena. "A Guide To The Various Parts Of A Flower." *Pansy Maiden: Flowers & Lifestyle.* May 24, 2021. https://www.pansymaiden.com/featured/a-guide-to-the-various-parts-of-a-flower/. Accessed Sept. 16, 2021.

Meredith, Leda. *Northeast Foraging.* Timberpress, Inc., 2014.

National Institutes of Health. National Library of Medicine. https://pubmed.ncbi.nlm.nih.gov. Accessed 4 May 2021.

National Library of Medicine. *National Center for Biotechnology Information.* PubMed. National Institutes of Health, www.pubmed.ncbi.nlm.nih.gov. Accessed 6 May. 2021.

North Carolina Extension Gardener Plant Toolbox. "*Viola cornuta.*" North Carolina Cooperative Extension. https://plants.ces.ncsu.edu/plants/viola-cornuta/. Accessed Sept. 16, 2021.

Ross, Rachel. "The Virtues of Violets: Health Benefits of Violets." *The Herbal Academy.* www.theherbalacademy.com/health-benefits-of-violets/. Accessed 27 Mar. 2021.

Rossi, Linda and Schuyler, Alfred E., "The Iconography of Plants Collected on the Lewis and Clark Expedition." *Great Plains Research: A Journal of Natural and Social Sciences.* www.digitalcommons.unl.edu/greatplainsresearch. 84, 1993, /84 Accessed 20 May 2021.

Rotterdam, Heidrun. "On pathology and on German etymology." Personal interview. Sept. 15, 2021.

Ruddick, Sara. "Maternal Thinking." *Feminist Studies* 6 (2), 1980, p 342.

Russ, Karen; Polemski, Bob; and Williamson, Joey. "Pansies and Johnny Jump-Ups." Factsheet HGIC 1169. *Home and Garden Information Center.* Clemson Cooperative Extension, Clemson University, Nov 19, 2020, www. hgic.clemson.edu/factsheet/pansies-and-johnny-jump-ups/?message=helpful &outcome=success. Accessed 31 Mar. 2021.

Science Learning Hub. "Plant Reproduction." The University of Waikato Te Whare Wānanga o Waikat, New Zealand. https://www.sciencelearn.org.nz/resources/100-plant-reprodurction. Accessed Sept. 17, 2021.

Shire Plants. "Viola sororia Albiflora." www.shireplants.co.uk/viola-sororia-albiflora. Accessed 31 Mar. 2021.

Weed, Susun. *New Menopausal Years: Alternative Approaches for Women 30-90, Rev..* (Orig. 1992.) Ash Tree Publishing, 2002.

-----. *Healing Wise.* Ash Tree Publishing, 1989.

Weldy, Troy, David Werier, and Andrew Nelson. 2021 *New York Flora Atlas.* [S. M. Landry and K. N. Campbell (original application development), USF Water Institute. University of South Florida]. New York Flora Association, Albany, New York. www.newyork.plantatlas.usf.edu/Genus.aspx?id=71. Accessed 20 May 2021.

Gail Wood Miller coaches, writes, speaks, draws, and does watercolors. She is a retired professor of English and English education, active in educational consulting. She often combines this as certified holistic health coach and ADHD coach, in her research and in her conference presentations. Gail specializes in working with women and children. She is a member of the Philadelphia Sketch Club and the Musconetcong Watercolor Group. She has studied at the Herzfeld School of Art, Cooper Union, the Minerva Foundation for Figure Drawing, and Salmagundi. She is indebted to Gert Coleman for introducing her to the wonderful world of herbs.

Viola cornuta. Gail Wood Miller

Long-stemmed Viola odorata. Gail Wood Miller

Poem to Violets

Jane Hawley Stevens

Let's acknowledge the flower of my state.
When violets emerge, I'll put away my skates.
The snow has melted, the ground has thawed,
It's enough to embrace Nature and applaud.

Is the value captured only in our sight?
No, infuse in tea, make syrup, or take a bite.
Pliny wrote of violets to ease a heartache,
And that was back in the year 28.

Athenians used violets to moderate anger and instill calm.
It has the presence of a sweet and wise grandmom.
Recently double-blind studies proved with asthma it eased.
Persian asthmatic children, while coughing and wheezing, the syrup
appeased.

We lost iconic herbalist, Jim Duke, who has the same birthday as Jane.
He said, "Eat 10 leaves a day to give health to the veins."
The signature leaf suggests the heart and love potions.
Capture the violet color in syrup or put in a lotion.

Known as heartsease with its heart-shaped leaves,
It blooms early giving food to butterflies and bees.
Beloved state flower of Wisconsin,
Pick them, dry them, but to keep color, store in a tin.

In meditation, the violet color transmutes.
Take a bad situation, visualize the best outcome, use the flower color, not
the roots.
Harvesting requires bending way down,
I think I will Namaste before I touch the ground.

Bios for Illustrators & Photographers

Susan Belsinger — see bio on page 6

Heather Cohen is a freelance graphic artist and web designer. She owns Small House Farm, a sustainable herb farm and seed sanctuary in Michigan.

Gert Coleman — see bio on page 86

Janice Cox — see bio on page 162

Karen England — see bio on page 130

Donna Frawley — see bio on page 138

Deborah Hall, artist, florist, and gardener loves and plays with plants and animals in Howard County, Maryland. She has been a longtime supporter of IHA's herbs of the year, sharing her plants, seeds, and knowledge.

Deb Jolly — see bio on page 51

Pat Kenny, retired medical illustrator, has been a member of the IHA since it was IHGMA. A member of HSA since 1979 and Vice President of IHA, Pat gives photo-illustrated herb talks and demos, neighborhood-to-nation. Pat's first illustration request that was not part of a human's anatomy was a watercolor painting of a violet. She was told by her father that the first time she tried to run away at the age of four, she was found picking violets in the nearby woods. She's been found in and out of the woods ever since.

Alicia Mann is a classically trained artist and metalsmith at Heritage Metalworks, LTD, in Downington, Pennsylvania. A graduate of Maryland College of Art, she integrates her interests in art and horticulture by growing flowers, herbs, vegetables, and fruit trees. Alicia's endearing violet artwork introduces the four sections of *Viola*.

Cooper Murrey — see bio on page 147

Marge Powell — see bio on page 213

Jane Stevens — see bio on page 218

Skye Suter — see bio on page 109

Phyllis Williams — see bio on page 150

Gail Wood Miller — see bio on page 225

Cover Credits

Front Cover:

Background image: Heather Cohen

Upper left: Susan Belsinger

Upper right: Susan Belsinger

Lower left: Susan Belsinger

Lower right: Susan Belsinger

Back Cover:

Left: Susan Belsinger

Center: Karen England

Right: Susan Belsinger

faces of purple

amidst heart-shaped foliage

violets riot

Susan Belsinger

Carpet of wild violets. *Susan Belsinger*

Celebrating 25 Years
of Herb of the Year™!

How the Herb of the Year™ is Selected

Every year since 1995, the International Herb Association has chosen an Herb of the Year™ to highlight. The Horticultural Committee evaluates possible choices based on their being outstanding in at least two of the three major categories: medicinal, culinary, or decorative. Many other herb organizations support the herb of the year selection and we work together to educate the public about these herbs during the year.

Herbs of the Year™: Past, Present and Future

1995	Fennel	2011	Horseradish
1996	Monarda	2012	Rose
1997	Thyme	2013	Elderberry
1998	Mint	2014	Artemisia
1999	Lavender	2015	Savory
2000	Rosemary	2016	Capsicum
2001	Sage	2017	Cilantro & Coriander
2002	Echinacea	2018	Humulus
2003	Basil	2019	Agastache
2004	Garlic	2020	Rubus
2005	Oregano & Marjoram	2021	Parsley
2006	Scented Geraniums	2022	Viola
2007	Lemon Balm	2023	Ginger
2008	Calendula	2024	Yarrow
2009	Bay Laurel	2025	Chamomile
2010	Dill		

Books available on www.iherb.org

Join the IHA

Associate with other herb businesses and like-minded folks, network and have fun while you are doing it!

Membership Levels:

$50 Individual Professional
$50 Affiliate Professional
$50 Post Secondary Student

Log onto www.iherb.org to see what we are all about!

Membership includes:

Your business information listed on www.iherb.org
Membership directory
Herb of the Year™ publication
Quarterly newsletters
Online herbal support
Discounts on conference fees
Promotional support for IHA's Herb of the Year program and
National Herb Week
Support for National Herb Day
Assocation with a network of diverse herbal businesses

CPSIA information can be obtained
at www.ICGtesting.com
Printed in the USA
BVHW090855050522
635995BV00058B/1277